At the Foot of the Cross

For ██████ and family,

"We have seen the true light."

At the Foot of the Cross

Lessons from Ukraine

An Interview with
Archbishop Sviatoslav Shevchuk

By John Burger

OSV

Our Sunday Visitor
Huntington, Indiana

Our Sunday Visitor Publishing Division
Our Sunday Visitor, Inc.
200 Noll Plaza
Huntington, IN 46750
1-800-348-2440

ISBN: 978-1-63966-027-8 (Inventory No. T2769)
eISBN: 978-1-63966-028-5
LCCN: 2022950161

Cover design: Tyler Ottinger
Cover art: Adobe Stock
Interior design: Amanda Falk

1. RELIGION—Christianity—Catholic.
2. HISTORY—Europe—Eastern.
3. RELIGION—Christian Church—History.

PRINTED IN THE UNITED STATES OF AMERICA

For the People of Ukraine

And for Charley, Barbara, and Ivan —
Eternal Memory!

Contents

Foreword

It seems that the decision to write a book about the Head of the Ukrainian Greek Catholic Church (UGCC) turned out to be truly providential: Today it is important for the world to understand the history of Ukrainian resistance to communism, because it contains the key to understanding the resistance to the current Russian aggression. And the fate of the main character of this book — Patriarch Sviatoslav Shevchuk — is a bridge between different eras: the communist persecution of the Church, its revival, and its response to various modern challenges, including the war.

However, first of all, I want to pay tribute to the author of the book: His introduction and comments impress with their truthfulness and accuracy. They are impressive because the world knows almost nothing about the history of Ukraine, and even more so about its religious history. So, if I did not know about John Burger's American citizenship, I could easily attribute the authorship of his text to some Ukrainian, well-versed in both Ukrainian and Western contexts. Therefore, readers of this book can safely trust the author's conclusions; they do not contradict the truth of life in any way.

I am glad that through this book the world will once again imagine the realities of the "catacomb" Church with secret listening through the "Radiola" of liturgies from the Vatican with shaded windows and blocked doors. And with Sviatoslav's "image of the underground priest — men coming at night." At that time, an ancient phenomenon was reproduced: When a person loses, for example, his sight, all his other sensations become acute. Therefore, when the usual celebration of liturgies in churches with all the accompanying elements was unavailable to Ukrainian Greek Catholics, a special sense of the presence of God was revealed to them. I know this phenomenon from the realities of imprisonment in Soviet labor camps, and therefore followed with great trust the story of His Beatitude Sviatoslav about the experience of faith in the underground "home" Church.

The mentioned phenomenon determined another feature of the "catacomb" UGCC: Its faithful were tightly isolated by the "iron curtain" from the post-war Church processes in the world. In particular, they did not receive the inspired Second Vatican Council, which opened the Church to the world. As His Beatitude Sviatoslav himself said about it, "they very often would not be able to follow all those worldwide ecumenical movements, or that openness to the modern world, because we were like a frozen Church, remembering the times before the Second World War as a golden time." But they experienced immersion in God, who came to them in the isolation of their underground. Because Christ is the first to do what he calls us to do: "I was ... in prison and you visited me" (Mt 25:35–36).

The child's eyes of little Sviatoslav noticed all the moral abomination of the official Soviet lies — and this must also be remembered to understand where the current abomination of Vladimir Putin's lies comes from. After all, the current Kremlin regime is a direct reincarnation of the communist regime, and both resembled the mockingbirds of Isaiah, who "made lies [their] refuge, / and in falsehood ... found a hiding place" (Is 28:15). However, this was one side of world reality. About the second — relativism in Western civilization — in one stroke, but very convincingly, John Burger himself wrote. And therefore, his conclusion about what we got as a result is absolutely accurate: "The very concept of truth has been called into question. Fake news, misinformation, disinformation, and conspiracy theories all take their toll on our understanding of truth."

It is amazing how strangely God worked with Sviatoslav, throwing him after his ordination to Argentina, then to Greece, then back to Ukraine. Truly, "God was good enough to test him in the different situations, with different external circumstances." And this prepared him for the main test, when he, the youngest of the UGCC bishops, was elected by the Synod of Bishops as the Head of the Church. It is no exaggeration to say that the whole Church was amazed, and there were certainly those faithful who doubted whether the Synod Fathers correctly read the will of the Holy Spirit. Therefore, it is a pity that His Beatitude Sviatoslav, out of modesty, does not talk extensively about that amazing moment in the cathedral of Naples, when he "was giving the relic back to the parish priest of the cathedral, [the blood of the most famous martyr of Naples] became liquid. It was considered a miracle, because normally it would happen only for special feasts." Such moments teach us humility, because they testify that we, humans, are unable to grasp the will of the Holy Spirit with our minds.

It is impossible to list all the topics touched upon in the dialogues of this book. It will be an excellent guide for everyone who wants to get acquainted with the vision of the current world through the eyes of a prominent Ukrainian and the Head of the Eastern Catholic Church in Ukraine — "a Ukrainian Church, but not a Church only for Ukrainians," as it is explained in the book. The reader will learn from it about the peculiarities of the Eastern Christian tradition and about the challenges associated with it, in particular about the challenge of married clergy. The reader will learn how strengthening the personal responsibility of people for the state of affairs in the country is the key to overcoming Soviet paternalism, and not only in the secular world, but also in the Church: "If I evangelize, the Church evangelizes. If I am faithful to my vocation, I make the Church faithful to her vocation."

However, I came across one place that seemed too politically correct to me. Answering the question about the role of the laity in the Church,

His Beatitude Sviatoslav answered truthfully, but not exhaustively. Truthfully, because who but Sviatoslav knows what an amazing role laymen played in the fact that the "catacomb" Church survived. Here he is absolutely right. However, he still bypassed the question about what *concerns* about the laity in the Church he sees. And I, as a layman of this Church, feel our weaknesses very well, so at the first moment I thought with interest: *And what will my patriarch say about them?* However, the next thought was a redeeming statement: *Maybe it's better that he didn't say anything about it.*

I pass over many important reflections of the patriarch about the Ukrainian Maidans — or, as they are otherwise called, the Ukrainian revolutions — and turn to his view on the mass invasion of Russian troops into Ukraine on February 24, 2022. He gave the readers a very accurate image: "For our people, in Ukraine and abroad, it would seem that the cross of Our Lord was abruptly thrust upon our shoulders from the very beginning of Great Lent, and we have already been carrying it not for a day or two, a week or two, but continuously, day and night."

The patriarch's conclusions are fresh — just "taken off the hot plate" of his heart. The valuable examples are the stories about liturgies in the Kyivan subway or about the sacrifice of individual people. However, among these reflections there is one that is especially dear to me. We Ukrainians suffer a lot when we hear calls today in some countries of the world to make compromises as soon as possible, make peace with the Russians and end this war. We suffer because no one wants peace as much as we do — we, the Ukrainians, who die every day in this cursed war. But we are terribly afraid that we will be forced into an imitative peace, which will give Putin a break and an opportunity to accumulate strength for a new war. After all, he has not yet achieved his main goal.

That is why it was so important for me to read the absolutely true and even prophetic words of the patriarch: "We are praying for peace, for an end of the war. But peace always has to be connected with truth and justice. An unjust and inauthentic peace would be the imitation of peace. My fear is that the very notion of peace in today's world can change its authentic meaning. Peace doesn't mean the simple absence of war. Peace means harmony, fullness of life. We look for victory over the very cause, which can cause new wars."

So, I fully share the hope of the author of this book that "as we read the pages ahead, we contemplate how His Beatitude's testimony might help us to get through our present darkness — whether personal or societal — and come into the Light."

Myroslav Marynovych,
Vice-Rector of the Ukrainian Catholic University in Lviv
Former Gulag prisoner (1977–1987)

Introduction

In late 2019 and early 2020, the American news media, the talking heads, and the political world were engulfed in the impeachment and Senate trial of US President Donald J. Trump. Trump was accused of exerting undue pressure on the president of Ukraine, Volodymyr Zelenskyy, to open an investigation into a political rival, Democratic presidential contender Joseph R. Biden Jr. Trump allegedly withheld important military assistance to Ukraine, which was defending itself against Russian aggression, unless Zelenskyy did his bidding.

In the end, the Republican-controlled Senate acquitted the president. Then, the novel coronavirus pandemic overshadowed just about everything, making "Ukrainegate" a distant memory.

Ukraine would come roaring back into the news in February 2022, as Russian President Vladimir Putin launched what he euphemistically called a "special military operation" in Ukraine. The unprovoked invasion and subsequent battles across Ukraine led to the deaths of thousands of troops on both sides, damaged a substantial amount of infrastructure, yielded a flow of refugees that reached biblical proportions, and sharply ratcheted up fears of World War III and nuclear holocaust.

People all over the world were captivated by news of the war. As in the case of Ukrainegate, the conflict made Americans — often thought of as being geographically illiterate — more familiar with this former Soviet republic. Prior to these events, many people might have assumed that Ukrainians are pretty much the same as Russians. Those paying attention might have learned that we no longer refer to the Eastern European country as "*The* Ukraine." Folks listening to National Public Radio or viewing PBS *NewsHour* learned how to pronounce the name *Volodymyr* (vo-lo-DIH-meer) and not confuse it with its Russian counterpart, Vladimir. Many news outlets updated their style books to refer to the nation's capital in the Ukrainian-preferred transliteration of *Kyiv*, rather than the Russian-style *Kiev*.

Granted, this was not the first time Ukraine was in the news, even in the US. Going back to 1986, there was the terrible nuclear accident at Chernobyl (an incident that received fresh treatment in an HBO miniseries that aired in May 2019). In 2004, there was the Orange Revolution, in which Ukrainians took to the streets protesting rigged election results. The *Euromaidan* protests in 2013–2014, which came to be known as the Revolution of Dignity, led to a massive rejection of the Russia-friendly president Viktor Yanukovych and affirmed Ukrainians' orientation toward the European Union. The events on the Maidan, Kyiv's central square, also led to Russia's manipulation of a local plebiscite in Crimea to leave Ukraine and become part of Russia, as well as the backing of separatist movements in Eastern Ukraine and a long-simmering conflict there.

A few months before the world learned about President Trump's infamous phone call with President Zelenskyy, I was sitting in the back seat of a black Volkswagen sedan, traveling from Kyiv to Lviv in Western Ukraine. Next to me was the head of the Ukrainian Greek Catholic Church, His Beatitude Sviatoslav Shevchuk, who was answering questions for this book. I had begun the interview the day before at the Patriarchal Residence in Kyiv, but because of an unforeseen schedule change, His Beatitude needed to be in Lviv and suggested that the daylong road trip be the setting for part two of the interview. A Basilian monk named

Brother Ipatii was driving, and His Beatitude's secretary, Fr. Oleh Oleksa, sat in the front passenger seat. Father Oleh was fielding phone calls for His Beatitude and interrupted our interview only for the most urgent of matters.

One of those calls came from the office of President-elect Zelenskyy, presumably to confirm the date and time of their upcoming meeting. Zelenskyy, who had portrayed a Ukrainian president in a television comedy series, had been elected the real president less than two weeks earlier and was setting up meetings with various civic and religious leaders ahead of his May 21 inauguration.

A few days later, Zelenskyy would be visiting the Patriarchal Residence to greet the head of the Ukrainian Greek Catholic Church.

For His Beatitude Sviatoslav, having a newly elected president calling on him in his own residence might still be somewhat surprising and unimaginable. But then, so have so many other events in his relatively young life. A couple of days after our interview, he turned forty-nine, and he had already lived through so much: the experience of being a Catholic in hiding, while growing up in a Soviet Ukraine that had outlawed his Church; studying for the priesthood in a secret seminary while at the same time preparing for life as an army medic; being chosen to study in Argentina (even as his country was still part of the Soviet Union) and later in Rome; being chosen to return to Argentina as a bishop; and finally, being elected at age forty as Major Archbishop of Kyiv-Halych, making him the leader of a worldwide Eastern Catholic Church, the largest in communion with Rome.

I too was somewhat surprised at where I found myself. As someone who had written for the Catholic press in the United States for a quarter of a century, I had developed a sense that most Catholic media focused almost solely on the *Roman*, or Western, Catholic experience and largely neglected the many Eastern Catholic Churches and their spirituality, traditions, and history. I had merely wanted to interview His Beatitude for the website I was working for, Aleteia, when he came to the United States in 2018. I did so, and because of the articles I wrote, a member of his staff, Fr. Volodymyr Malchyn, mentioned to me that he and his colleagues for some time had discussed their hopes that someone could write an English-language biography of His Beatitude. Father Volodymyr asked if I'd be interested.

My first impulse was to ensure that I had complete editorial freedom over such a project. "You shouldn't expect to see a draft of my book before it goes to press," I told him, explaining that it was important that this not be seen as some kind of public relations effort for His Beatitude or the Ukrainian Catholic Church; otherwise, it would lack credibility. His Beatitude agreed to the terms, and in fact, I learned later that he was not so gung-ho about the project when it was first proposed to him.

"When I heard about the idea, I was not happy, I have to say," he told me when we sat down at his residence in Kyiv, "because I think some sort of biography should be written at the end of someone's life. But I'm only in the beginning, and I'm not the one who could be interesting for such a project."

But he agreed in the end because "I understood that maybe this book would be not about my humble person but on behalf of our Church, which for many years was considered a silent Church, especially in the time of the Soviet Union. And step by step, that Church, because of its sufferings but also today's vibrancy, is trying to have a voice, to speak up loudly on behalf of the suffering people of Ukraine."

Rather than a biography, he agreed to cooperate in a book-length interview. He had already done two of them, in fact: *Dimmi la verità*, with Italian theologian Paolo Asolan, in 2018 (with a preface by Cardinal Christoph Schönborn of Vienna), and *Dialogue Heals Wounds*, with Krzysztof Tomasik, the editor of the Polish Catholic News Agency, in 2019.

And here I was, in a country I had never thought of visiting, peppering His Beatitude with a long list of questions I had developed in part from my own interest, experience, and research, and in part after interviewing a number of experts and observers, members of the Ukrainian Greek Catholic Church, Orthodox theologians, historians, and others.

And, as His Beatitude took some of the phone calls, I watched the landscape breeze by: the black soil that was world-famous for making Ukraine the breadbasket of Europe, the onion domes of churches gracing every little town and village we passed through. I thought of the centuries of history that this land had witnessed and all the witnesses of the Christian Faith who had stood against oppressors from abroad.

***

As will become clearer, this is not a book only about Ukraine, or even the Ukrainian Greek Catholic Church. But Ukraine is its starting point, so some background is in order.

Ukraine has been a battleground, both literal and metaphorical, over much of her history. I can only touch the very surface of that history here. Looking back one hundred years or so, for example, Ukrainians have suffered through such ignominies as a famine engineered by Soviet dictator Joseph Stalin; the carving up of their land by Poland and Russia; the invasion and occupation of the western part of the country by Nazi Germany and the slaughter of its Jews by the *Einsatzgruppen*; and the long control of the country by the Soviet Union and its manipulation of Ukrainians' spiritual life.

And, of course, the invasion by neighboring Russia in 2022. The flow of refugees toward Poland and other western countries was nothing new for Ukraine. As in the histories of other nations, events and trends and harsh conditions in the past led to waves of emigration to Western Europe, North and South America, Australia, and other places. Ukrainian emigrants might not have been able to bring much with them in the way of material goods, but many brought their ingenuity and industriousness — and that precious spiritual life. The Church, whether Orthodox or Catholic, was such a vital part of the fabric of life in the old country that it had to be replicated in the new.

Today, in very broad terms, Ukraine's religious makeup is largely Christian, with minorities of Jews and Muslims. The eastern part of the country is more Orthodox, while Western Ukraine has a higher number of Catholics. To untrained eyes and ears, one would hardly notice the difference. In the western part, aside from a small number of Latin Catholics, the religious scene in the region is dominated by Greek Catholics, whose Byzantine liturgy is basically the same one used by the Ukrainian (and Russian) Orthodox. Most priests are married and have families, just like their Orthodox brethren.

Christianity is thought to have arrived in the land now known as Ukraine as early as apostolic times. Saint Andrew is said to have visited the hills of Kyiv and declared, "God will shine the light upon these hills: A great city will rise here, and the Lord will erect many churches there and enlighten the Rus' lands with Church baptism."

But Kyivan Rus', the medieval kingdom the original Volodymyr ruled, was largely pagan until the late tenth century. It is said that this prince was looking for an appropriate religion to unite his people, so he sent emissaries to various realms to advise him about which would be best. It wasn't until his legates came back from Greek-speaking Constantinople, telling him of an amazing religious experience they had in the Cathedral of Hagia Sophia, that he was moved to embrace one particular tradition. Describing the Divine Liturgy to Volodymyr, the men exclaimed, "We knew not whether we were in heaven or on earth."

Volodymyr accepted baptism for himself and his people in the year 988. The Church of Kyiv thus became subject to the Great Church of Constantinople. Volodymyr's son Prince Yaroslav the Wise built Kyiv's own version of the mother church, Hagia Sophia, in the early eleventh century. It still stands today but was seriously threatened by Russian bombardment in 2022. Like its protégé in Istanbul until it was converted into a mosque in 2020, it is a museum, though the Orthodox still serve Divine Liturgies there.

Sadly, divisions arose in the Church, including the so-called Great Schism of 1054 between Rome and Constantinople. The Mongol invasion of Kyiv in 1240 led to the Church's diminished status and the development of the Church of Moscow. The Russian Orthodox Church in time absorbed Ukrainian Orthodoxy, and Ukrainians struggled through the centuries to assert their cultural and spiritual independence, to varying degrees of success. To them, Kyiv was the sacred place of their nation's baptism, while to Russians, "Kiev" became known as the Mother of All Russian Cities.

As for the Western Church, struggling with its own schisms among the Protestants, the most successful attempts to restore communion with the East came in the late sixteenth to mid-seventeenth centuries.

The Union of Brest brought several Ukrainian Orthodox bishops into communion with the Bishop of Rome, whose primacy they recognized. Rome in turn guaranteed that their Byzantine liturgy, calendar of feast days, and practices, such as ordaining married men to the priesthood, would continue.

What resulted from this agreement, in 1596, was what was first called the Uniate Church and today is known as the Ukrainian Greek Catholic Church. Fifty years later, in 1646, the Council of Uzhhorod brought several more bishops into communion with Rome, resulting in what is now known as the Ruthenian Greek Catholic Church. Its spiritual home is in the Carpathian Mountains of southwestern Ukraine and several neighboring lands.

These two Churches maintained their people's Eastern Christian spirituality and traditions as the tectonic plates of the geopolitical world around them shifted and crashed against one another. In some places, borders have changed so often that locals have found the history a source of humor. One story concerns a man in Uzhhorod, a city in modern-day Western Ukraine. One day, the man's grandson asked him, "Grandpa, how many countries have you lived in?" "Well," the man responded, "I was born in the Austro-Hungarian Empire. Then, I studied in Czechoslovakia. After college, I went to work in Hungary. I met a young lady and got married in the Soviet Union. And finally, I retired in Ukraine."

"Gee, Grandpa, you've traveled around a lot!" said the impressionable lad.

"Not at all, son!" the elder replied. "I've never left Uzhhorod!"

Regarding another city, on the other side of the Carpathian Mountains, someone wrote on Twitter, "You can be born in the Austro-Hungarian Empire, educated in Poland, married under the Third Reich, work and retire in the USSR and draw your pension in Ukraine and never have left the town … LVIV."

Sviatoslav Yuri Shevchuk can attest to this. Born in the Western Ukrainian city of Stryi on May 5, 1970, he was the first child of Yuri Ivanovych Shevchuk and Vira Vasylivna Krokis Shevchuk. He grew up hearing stories of his parents, grandparents, and great-grandparents, who had to deal with the demands of changing regimes, shifting political situations, and the conflicts of twentieth-century Eastern Europe.

His maternal grandfather, Vasyl Krokis, was born in Galicia in what was then part of the Austro-Hungarian Empire. It later came under Polish rule, and Vasyl was recruited into the Polish Army a year before the Germans invaded in 1939. He ended up in a concentration camp in Wroclaw. Galicia fell under Nazi occupation in 1941, and Vasyl's future wife was sent to Wroclaw to serve as what the Germans called an *Ostarbeiter*, a "worker from the East." The two met, fell in love, and escaped together back to Galicia, hiding in a family home near Stryi.

Sviatoslav's grandmother — the *Ostarbeiter* — had two brothers, the younger of whom was recruited into the Soviet Army, and the older of whom, a soldier in the Ukrainian resistance organization known as the UPA, was killed fighting Soviet control of Western Ukraine. In 1945, because of this connection to the resistance, the grandmother and her husband and parents were almost deported to Siberia. But a letter came just in time from the younger brother in the Soviet Army, then serving in Berlin. The family was set free, but by the time they got back to their house, they found that it had been almost completely looted.

***

Life for religious believers in post-war Ukraine was not easy, but it was especially challenging for Ukrainian Greek Catholics like the Krokises and Shevchuks. While the Soviet regime tended to tolerate the Orthodox Church (which came under the Patriarchate of Moscow and could be manipulated by the state), and even allowed certain Roman Catholic churches to stay open, the Kremlin saw the Ukrainian Greek Catholic Church as a spiritual power closely allied with Ukrainian nationalism. Striking first at the head of the Church in expectation that the body would soon be thrown into leaderless confusion, the Soviets in 1945 arrested the Metropolitan of Lviv, Josyf Slipyj, and all the bishops, as well as many priests.

The following year, the NKVD, forerunner to the KGB, with the help of sympathetic Greek Catholic priests, orchestrated a Church council that voted to nullify the Union of Brest and return the Church to the fold of Orthodoxy. Following the vote of this so-called Pseudo-Sobor of Lviv, the Ukrainian Greek Catholic Church was formally dissolved. It no longer existed — at least on paper. Churches were converted into theaters, funeral homes, or storage houses for chemicals or books. Some were turned into Orthodox churches. One ended up housing a museum of atheism.

"The Soviets suspected the Catholic Church as a whole of doing the bidding of the Vatican and the Western powers," writes Serhii Plokhy in *The Gates of Europe: A History of Ukraine*.[1] "All institutional, religious, and cultural links with the West had to be cut."

But the faithful in large part were not willing to meekly submit to this scheme. While priests and bishops in prison refused to convert to Orthodoxy, in spite of torture and with some paying for their fidelity with their lives, many of the lay faithful found ways to continue practicing the sacramental life of the Church clandestinely.

It was not only the Divine Liturgy and the sacraments that were suddenly at a premium; it was education as well. The Church could not carry on her catechesis of the young openly, and at the same time, public education, which was the only option for anyone, promoted the regime's political, historical, and spiritual views.

"When it was Christmas, we never had a holiday," Oksana Rybak, a nurse now living in New York, told me, remembering her days as a schoolgirl in the 1970s and 1980s. "You have to be at school, no matter what. Easter is always on Sunday, so they always did something so you would have to be at school that day. If you didn't go, you'd have to give them proof that you were sick or something. Because Easter is mostly in April, it's the month they celebrate Lenin's birth, so they always had something connected with Lenin, like a conference or cleaning land in Lenin's name or something."

Some Greek Catholics did attend local Orthodox churches, simply to be able to receive the sacraments and continue some kind of practice of the Faith. After all, although they have not been in communion with one another for a millennium, the Catholic and Orthodox Churches both

---

1. From *The Gates of Europe* by Serhii Plokhy, copyright © 2015. Reprinted by permission of Basic Books, an imprint of Hachette Book Group, Inc.

trace the lineage of their bishops directly to the apostles, so they both have valid bishops and priests and therefore valid sacraments.

The sacraments are the visible signs of God's grace, and for faithful Catholics and Orthodox they are vital lifelines for their spiritual lives. Baptism is the gateway into the Church, and even functionaries for the Soviet regime in Ukraine and other parts of the USSR sometimes secretly brought their babies to a priest to be baptized. Confession is the practice by which a sinner humbly approaches God through the priest for forgiveness and absolution. Marriage and priestly ordination are two sacraments in which one's vocation in life is blessed.

But the most commonly received sacrament is the Eucharist, or holy Communion, instituted by Jesus at the Last Supper the night before he suffered and died on the cross. When Jesus took, broke, and blessed bread, and likewise blessed a cup of wine, and said, "This is my body, this is my blood, which will be given up for you," he gave it to his disciples and commanded them to "do this in memory of me." Priests down through the ages have been faithful to that command. The lay followers of Christ, heedful of Jesus' promise that "whoever eats my flesh and drinks my blood has eternal life, and I will raise him on the last day" (Jn 6:54), have likewise been faithful to receiving the sacrament.

Those Greek Catholics who could not or were not willing to attend Orthodox churches or even the Roman Catholic churches that were allowed to be open sometimes did what they could to continue this sacred tradition. There are numerous reports of priests conducting secret liturgies in people's apartments or even in wooded areas, away from the prying eyes of both unsympathetic neighbors and NKVD/KGB agents. Common household items, such as a glass goblet, served as sacramental vessels and could easily be put back on a shelf if there was an ominous knock at the door.

It was in this milieu that Sviatoslav Shevchuk grew up. The Shevchuks had ties to priests in the "underground Church." His paternal grandfather's home, in Broshniv-Osada, was one of those places for secret liturgies. His maternal grandfather, Vasyl Krokis, a tailor by profession, sewed vestments for underground priests.

But his immediate family, like many others, often had to content themselves mostly with listening in secret to broadcasts of the Divine Liturgy on Vatican Radio. In the Shevchuk home in Stryi, it was a typical Sunday practice to gather the family, close the doors, and cover the windows and stand in front of family icons and some candles, tuning into Vatican Radio on the *Radiola* and praying the liturgy along with the broadcast. It was much like the way many Catholics around the world would "attend" Mass when the COVID-19 pandemic forced the closure of churches in 2020. Like 2020, Catholics in Ukraine had to make a "spiritual Communion" — a prayer beseeching Christ to come into their hearts in a spiritual way — as they had no priest there to consecrate the bread and wine that would be the physical sacrament. As Catholics in 2020 were dispensed from the moral obligation to attend Mass on Sunday in person because of the pandemic, Catholics in Soviet Ukraine were assured by the announcer on Vatican Radio that listening devoutly to the broadcast liturgy, under the circumstances, could be their way of fulfilling their Sunday obligation.

Transmission of the Divine Liturgy over Vatican Radio was "an outstanding spiritual event," Sviatoslav told me.

But while it was not dangerous for Americans and others in the West to view a livestreamed Mass through Facebook or YouTube in 2020, it was risky for Ukrainians in the 1970s and 1980s to be discovered listening to such broadcasts. At the very least, one could lose a job or opportunities for education.

Sviatoslav's parents both had jobs in sensitive areas, so this was a special concern. His father worked for the railroad, which was considered part of the strategic communications in the Cold War–era Soviet Union. He was an engineer for radio communication and had access to sensitive information. His mother taught in the town's music school. As such, she was part of the Soviet Union's team of educators responsible to form new generations in Soviet thought.

Anyone found out to be a faithful Ukrainian Greek Catholic could not be trusted with such responsibilities.

For Catholics, it is in situations like these that the value of the family's role as "domestic church," as the Second Vatican Council called it, becomes most apparent. Sviatoslav's family was certainly that, as they worshiped together, as they lived out the moral teachings of the Church and strove to live virtuous lives, as the elders exhibited their fidelity to a private prayer life, and as they taught the Faith explicitly to the younger members — Sviatoslav and his younger brother, Vsevolod.

"I understood that their relationship with God for them was very important," Sviatoslav recalled. "That was almost the cornerstone of their way of being. And maybe a small kid doesn't understand what they are doing, but he understands very well if they are doing something important or not."

Years later, as head of the Ukrainian Greek Catholic Church, during a meeting of the Synod of Bishops in Rome, he commented on Vatican Radio, "I received my Christian Faith in my family, and actually, in the former Soviet Union, Christian families were real *ecclesiae domesticae* [domestic churches]. ... This was the 'home church,' where a priest could come and celebrate sacraments, where I learned a basic notion of Christian Faith from my grandmother, and even in those circumstances, I learned how to pray, how to worship, how to live my life according to the Christian moral principles."

He witnessed those underground priests serving the clandestine community. Like his mother, he had musical talent, learning the violin and developing a rich tenor voice (he still plays violin in his free time). He accompanied a deacon to a secret nighttime liturgy in which they sang the psalms over a recently deceased person, while the family mourned in the home. A priest noticed how well Sviatoslav sang — so important to a Church whose liturgy is mostly sung.

Over time, Sviatoslav began to hear a call in his own heart to serve this underground community in a special way. On a family visit to a famous Orthodox shrine, he had a moving prayer experience before a famous icon of the Virgin Mary. In time, he was visiting an underground seminary, making preparations to study for the priesthood.

But after his youthful studies in the schools of Stryi, he moved out of his family home at age fifteen to attend a medical school in the city of Boryslav, less than an hour away by car. Here, he would study to be a *feldscher*, a field medic. He excelled in his medical studies, even as he was studying theology in secret, traveling to a secret seminary in the Carpathian Mountains to obtain contraband books which he would take back to his rented room in Boryslav and copy by hand late at night.

According to law, all young men had to serve in the Soviet military. Sviatoslav did so for two years — in the army, as a medic — but had to delay his priestly vocation. Once he completed his military service, however, the Church was coming out of the underground, thanks in part to Mikhail Gorbachev's opening-up policies of *glasnost* and *perestroika*, and in part to Pope John Paul II's pressure on the Soviet leader.

Finally, Sviatoslav, and many others, were able to attend the newly reopened seminary, which, along with the Ukrainian Greek Catholic Church, had been suppressed for decades.

***

An opportunity arose for Sviatoslav and a few other students to do part of their studies in Argentina, where a Ukrainian immigrant community needed priests. There he earned a degree in philosophy and learned to speak Spanish. He was ordained a priest in June 1994, but the seminary in Lviv needed good professors. His bright mind, as well as his experience in Argentina, made him a natural candidate for higher studies in Rome. After all, someone who has learned Spanish can more easily learn Italian.

He finished a doctorate in moral theology at the Angelicum in Rome in 1999, defending his dissertation in the very same room where Karol Wojtyła had defended his in 1948, and returned to teach at the seminary in Lviv. In 2002, he became personal secretary to the head of the Ukrainian Greek Catholic Church, Cardinal Lubomyr Husar, and in 2007, rector of the seminary.

But in 2009, South America was calling again, this time for a bishop. The Synod of the Ukrainian Greek Catholic Church elected Sviatoslav to fill the role, and he found himself once again on a plane to Buenos Aires.

At the time, Cardinal Husar explained the decision this way:

As a student, Father Sviatoslav was one of those whom the at-that-time eparchial bishop of the UGCC in Argentina, Andrés (Sapelak), invited to this country to study theology there and, consequently, there were pastors for the faithful of our Church in Argentina. At this time, he learned Spanish and got to know the culture of this country. Now when we were choosing a candidate for a bishop for the Greek-Catholics of Argentina, the choice, considering this primary idea about his ministering in this country, came down precisely on Father Sviatoslav.

He added that the new bishop would do a good job in finding priests to serve there.

When Bishop Sviatoslav returned to Argentina, another cardinal was waiting to welcome him. Jorge Mario Bergoglio, the Roman Catholic Archbishop of Buenos Aires, introduced him at a meeting of the country's bishops' conference. Bishop Sviatoslav remembers that the prelates looked at the thirty-eight-year-old Ukrainian as if they were asking who this altar boy was. Bishop Sviatoslav found Cardinal Bergoglio to be like a father figure to him, guiding him through some difficulties and helping him learn how to be a bishop more as a servant-leader than a prince.

He would have been happy remaining in Argentina with his Ukrainian flock, but in 2011, in an unprecedented move, the aging patriarch of the Ukrainian Church, Cardinal Husar, who was already going blind, decided to step down from his role as major archbishop. Some forty bishops of the Church — both from Ukraine and from the "diaspora" — were summoned to a special electoral meeting in Lviv. Acting as the Synod of the Church, they elected the youngest among them, Bishop Sviatoslav of the Eparchy of the Protection of the Most Holy Mother of God in Buenos Aires, Argentina, about a month and a half shy of his forty-first birthday. A young patriarch, yes, but so were some of his predecessors when they stepped into the role. Andrei Sheptytsky, arguably the greatest leader of the Ukrainian Church in the twentieth century, was thirty-six when he was installed in 1901.

Two days before the synod was to begin, Bishop Sviatoslav ordained his brother, Vsevolod, eleven years his junior, a priest. Two days after the election, the Holy See confirmed the choice of the Ukrainian Synod of Bishops.

On a side note, two years later, in an almost unprecedented move, the aging Bishop of Rome, Pope Benedict XVI, decided to step down, and all the cardinals of the Catholic Church were summoned to the Vatican for a special electoral meeting, known as a conclave. Cardinal Jorge Mario Bergoglio of the Archdiocese of Buenos Aires, Argentina, was elected to succeed Pope Benedict.

"Many of us said, 'Can't the Roman Church do anything original?'" commented Fr. Andriy Chirovsky, former director of the Metropolitan Andrey Sheptytsky Institute of Eastern Christian Studies in Toronto.

***

Two terms which we have already used, and which will come up again, merit at least a brief mention: *patriarch* and *major archbishop*. There has been much controversy about why the Vatican has not yet responded to the request of several successive leaders of the Ukrainian Greek Catholic Church, beginning with Cardinal Josyf Slipyj, to grant the leader of this *sui iuris* Church the title of patriarch. After all, other Eastern Catholic Church leaders — the Maronite, Melkite, Syriac, Chaldean, and Coptic — are referred to in this way. A discussion of this would require a whole book. His Beatitude Sviatoslav expresses his thoughts about it in this book.

Suffice it to say that in the present volume, the terms will be used somewhat interchangeably. In the Divine Liturgy, he is prayed for as "Our blessed Patriarch Sviatoslav," and in common parlance, adherents of the Church refer to him as patriarch. His official *curriculum vitae* refers to him as "His Beatitude Sviatoslav Shevchuk, Father and Head of the Ukrainian Greek Catholic Church." He does not call himself a patriarch, but what else is a patriarch than a father and head, whether of a family, a nation, or of a Church?

His Beatitude Sviatoslav was enthroned on March 27, 2011, on what was in the Byzantine Church the Sunday of the Exaltation of the Cross. The ceremony took place in the yet-unfinished Cathedral of the Resurrection in Kyiv, which his predecessor, Lubomyr, had begun after moving the seat of the Church from Lviv. Sviatoslav was thus the first Ukrainian Greek Catholic primate to be enthroned in Kyiv since the eighteenth century.

"In the twentieth century, our Church went with its Savior to the end — unto the complete liquidation on its native land and death, it seemed," Sviatoslav said in his homily. "Yet this death of hundreds of thousands of our laity, clergy, monks, and nuns, with our episcopate in the lead, was a death on the cross, and therefore life-giving. Our parents, grandparents, and ancestors showed — through us, their descendants, and through us, to an independent Ukraine — the strength and invincibility of the honest and life-giving Cross of the Lord."

He referred to members of his Church as "heirs of Volodymyr's baptism."

And he became heir to a long line of primates who had led a Church through times of trial, division, repression, and new growth. As he took the helm, the Church was still enjoying her new freedom, still training an impressive number of seminarians, and still expanding to new parts of the world because of migration. In Ukraine and around the world, the Church claims more than seven and a half million adherents.

But just what is Sviatoslav's role as head of the Church? An article posted at the website of the Ukrainian Greek Catholic Church (www .ugcc.ua), put it this way:

> The Head and Father of our particular Church is both symbol and servant of her global unity, communion, and development. We see this illustrated magnificently in the examples of service given by the Venerable Metropolitan Andrey Sheptytsky and Confessor of Faith Josyf Slipyj. The Head of the Church presides over the Synod of Bishop[s] and its activity. It is he who convokes the Synod and Patriarchal Assemblies-Sobors.[2] He watches over the development of each eparchy [diocese] and serves to ensure that its needs are met. He proclaims synodal decisions and Church laws, which thus acquire canonical force. At the same time he also is guarantor of the full and visible communion of our Church with the successor of St. Peter, and has the right to speak fully on her behalf. He is, in fact, a servant-minister of this unity-in-love of all parts of our Church. The Head

---

2. This is a meeting that includes the bishops, priests, religious, and faithful of the Church from all continents.

of our Church is given the particular task of pastoral care over all the faithful of our Church, especially over those who reside outside its pastoral structures. In order that this care be provided in an adequate and timely fashion, he is called to promote the creation of suitable pastoral centers, and further, the creation of new ecclesial structures should this be required by the good of our faithful. He has particular care over the liturgical life of our Church and ensures uniformity in the celebration of Divine worship worldwide. But above all, he is called to be a faithful and sincere brother to his fellow bishops and a good spiritual father for the entire Church community.[3]

Sviatoslav brings with him a truly *catholic*, or universal, approach to his role. He is proud to be Galician, and he loves his homeland dearly. He celebrates the Divine Liturgy faithfully and with love for the traditions reaching back to Constantinople. And he does so fully conscious of the price paid for religious liberty by so many martyrs of the past and other witnesses, including some in his own family and among his teachers.

But he also consciously works to make his ecclesial communion a Church for all who feel attracted by it to worship God in this way.

"We are a Ukrainian Church," he often says, "but we are not a Church only for Ukrainians."

And it's true. In the twenty-first century, when there is often so much choice in life and so much ease in travel and freedom to follow one's heart, Ukrainian parishes in North America, for example, that once were a bulwark of Eastern European immigrants, are now seeing many members who are from various ethnic backgrounds, whether they be white Anglo-Americans, Hispanic, African-American, or Chinese.

As Hispanic immigration has propped up many Roman Catholic parishes in North America that have seen dwindling attendance, so too an influx of non-Ukrainians may be what's needed to save parishes where the older generations of Slavic immigrants have moved on. Sviatoslav

---

3. Full text available at Synod of Bishops of the Ukrainian Greek-Catholic Church 2019, "Communion and Unity in the Life and Ministry of the Ukrainian Greek-Catholic Church," Archeparchy of Philadelphia Ukrainian Catholic Church, September 24, 2019, https://ukrarcheparchy.us/church-news/communion-and-unity-in-the-life-and-ministry-of-the-ukrainian-greek-catholic-church.

would only celebrate that development. He has pushed to make old, staid Ukrainian parishes more welcoming. He initiated a program called The Vibrant Parish, helping the faithful understand that the parish is a community of communities and the place where one meets the living Christ.

For many newcomers, it is the beauty of the ancient Byzantine liturgy that draws them and keeps them, as well as the ethereal music and rich icons, the spirituality and asceticism by which Eastern Christians search for God. This, combined with the witness of the Ukrainian "Martyr Church" and its lessons for today, and the verve of its young leader who is not shy about commenting on so many issues facing mankind today, can only be welcome elements in a world that sometimes seems to be falling into so much darkness.

In addition to being a year in which Ukraine enjoyed new attention on the part of Americans, thanks to the investigation into "Ukrainegate," 2019 was also the year in which the world marked the thirtieth anniversary of the "fall" of the Berlin Wall. There was a day or two of nostalgic reporting in the media, with photos of the night when hordes of Germans stood on the wall. But like Trump's troubles fading into the past only to be replaced by the coronavirus, the Iron Curtain too was soon forgotten.

On the other hand, socialism seems to be getting more popular in the West, thanks in part to some American political leaders, but also to generations of college students graduating with perhaps a rosy view of that system. This while the percentage of *Nones* goes up year by year — those who would check the "None" box on a survey when asked, "To which religious group do you belong?" The rates of major depression, anxiety, and suicide are also up. Years and years of being lectured to be tolerant of all kinds of lifestyle choices have given many people pause before making any kind of black-and-white statement or judgment. The very concept of truth has been called into question. Fake news, misinformation, disinformation, and conspiracy theories all take their toll on our understanding of truth.

It is for all these reasons that I believe that the recent history of Ukraine, the dramatic story of the Greek Catholic Church (particularly its experience of crucifixion and resurrection under the Soviet Union), and the moving story of one Ukrainian in particular merit our attention.

All three of these — nation, Church, and priest-patriarch — have gone through a period of darkness and come out again into the light. Let us listen to their story, told through the eyes, the memory, and the hopes of Sviatoslav Yuri Shevchuk.

The question-and-answer format that makes up most of this book is based on various interviews I had with His Beatitude: in Baltimore in August 2018; in Ukraine in May 2019; in Philadelphia in December 2019; and by telephone in the midst of the war of 2022. I have collated and edited them into what I hope is a readable, seamless discussion covering his own life experience, his work in the Church, and his views on the challenges facing the Church and the world today.

I would humbly suggest that as we read the pages ahead, we contemplate how His Beatitude's testimony might help us to get through our present darkness — whether personal or societal — and come into the Light.

1

Pastoring in Wartime Kyiv

The first explosions were heard before dawn on February 24, 2022. Russia was hitting military targets around Ukraine, including near the capital, Kyiv, with cruise missiles.

What was happening was unbelievable. This was Europe in the twenty-first century, and a major world power was invading a neighboring country — one that was much smaller and which had not attacked the larger one or provoked it in any way.

In many ways, though, it was not a surprise. There were danger signals going back at least several months. In the spring of 2021, Russia began massing troops along its border with Ukraine, saying it was for military exercises. That summer, Russian President Vladimir Putin published a five thousand–word essay on the historical and spiritual unity of Russia and Ukraine, basically arguing that Ukraine was an integral part of Russia. He had once commented that the breakup of the Soviet Union, which he had served in his youth as a KGB agent, was the "biggest geopolitical catastrophe of the century."

By February 2022, the number of Russian troops swelled to some one hundred and ninety thousand, not only along Ukraine's eastern border, but also along its northern border with Russia and neighboring Belarus, an ally of Russia. Troops were also being moved into Transnistria, a Russia-backed breakaway region of Moldova to Ukraine's southwest, and into Crimea, the Ukrainian peninsula Russia had begun to occupy in 2014. The Russian Navy increased its presence in the Black Sea, to the south.

Ukraine was being surrounded. And yet, Putin continued to insist that he had no intention of invading.

Ukrainians, both in their country and living abroad, pointed out that Russia had already invaded. Following the Maidan revolution of 2014, when the Russia-friendly Ukrainian president Viktor Yanukovych was forced out of office and fled to Russia, Putin orchestrated a takeover of Crimea. Soon, Russia-backed separatists in the Eastern Ukrainian oblasts of Donetsk and Luhansk, in a region known as the Donbas (the Donets coal basin), began a struggle for independence from Ukraine. Their conflict with the Ukrainian military, which simmered for eight years, claimed some fourteen thousand lives. Years of negotiations never resolved the issue.

Both Crimea and Donbas were considered as violations of the 1994 Budapest Memorandum. As a former republic of the Soviet Union, Ukraine had been left with a stockpile of nuclear weapons. In exchange for giving up that arsenal, Russia, the United States, and the United Kingdom signed an agreement guaranteeing Ukraine's sovereignty. Russia reneged on that when Putin took over Crimea.

Now, in 2022, Putin, who continued to deny any plans to invade Ukraine, demanded that certain threats against Russian security be reversed. He saw those threats to include the expansion of the North Atlantic Treaty Organization (NATO) to include former Warsaw Pact countries. The alliance also had promised that Ukraine could someday join. Western powers, whose intelligence operatives increasingly confirmed Putin's plans for an invasion, made new negotiation attempts with the Russian government and prepared a set of sanctions to try to persuade Putin to change his mind.

NATO refused to consider scaling back or rescinding its Ukrainian invitation. Western intelligence warned that Russia would orchestrate a pretext to invade, deploying a "false flag" operation, most likely in the Donbas, simulating what appeared to be an attack on innocent Russian-speaking civilians in one of the separatist areas, so that Russian forces would be compelled to respond. Shelling along the front line in Donetsk and Luhansk increased significantly, and Putin sent in "peacekeeping" forces. On Monday, February 21, the Russian Parliament voted to recognize the independence of the Donetsk People's Republic and the Luhansk People's Republic. It also voted to authorize Putin to use the military outside of Russia, and the separatists called on Putin for help in defending themselves against the Ukrainian military.

Ukrainians went to bed Wednesday night, February 23, with a great sense of unease. "How can I sleep tonight?" someone in Kyiv tweeted.

By four thirty the next morning, what had been unimaginable in early twenty-first-century Europe came to pass. Putin made an early-morning televised address saying the Russian military was conducting a "special military operation" in Ukraine. It would turn into the most significant land war in Europe since the Second World War. In subsequent days and nights, Russian bombing would increase, bringing the war closer to civilian populations and terrorizing cities like Kyiv. Western governments had supplied military equipment to Ukraine, but NATO could not send in troops to help repel the aggression, as Ukraine was not a member of the alliance. President Joseph Biden assured the American people that he would not send troops into the country. Western allies ramped up sanctions, and Putin ratcheted up his threats, even putting Russia's nuclear forces on high alert.

Among the thousands of Kyivans taking refuge in basements, bomb shelters, subway stations, and underground parking garages was His Beatitude Sviatoslav Shevchuk, a highly regarded religious leader in Ukraine. Officially the Major Archbishop of Kyiv-Halych, he is widely referred to as Patriarch of the Ukrainian Greek Catholic Church. His residence is at the Cathedral of the Resurrection of Christ, on the east side of the Dnipro River.

On the first night of bombing, he moved down into the basement of that cathedral and subsequently moved to an undisclosed location in Kyiv. Like other religious leaders in Ukraine — bishops and pastors — he refused to leave the capital for safer territory. He said he would stay with his people.

Even as the attack on Kyiv intensified, His Beatitude published a daily video message on social media, addressed to the faithful of the Ukrainian Greek Catholic Church, both in Ukraine and in the rest of the world. Seated in what appeared to be a somewhat ornate chair in front of drapery, the fifty-one-year-old prelate was dressed in a simple black cassock, wearing his *panaghia*, an icon-graced medallion that is similar to a pectoral cross for Western bishops, around his neck. He had a neat haircut and a graying beard. He seemed at times to be trying to appear confident, though his voice shook somewhat. But he had lost none of his enthusiasm for preaching the Gospel and retained a youthful spirit.

Because of the government-ordered curfew, Sviatoslav said in his message on February 27, the first Sunday since the invasion began, that Ukrainians were not able to get to church. In some cases, local pastors were going into bomb shelters and subway stations to perform the liturgical rites among the people who were taking refuge there.

"We survived yet another horrible night," he said. "But after night there comes day. There is morning. After darkness, there comes light, just as after death there comes resurrection, which we all today radiantly celebrate."

His eyes looked heavy, as if he had not been getting much sleep.

According to the Church's liturgical calendar, it was Cheesefare Sunday, the last of several preparatory Sundays before the Great Fast, which Christians in the West call Lent.

> On this Sunday we will celebrate the presence among us, the presence here in Ukraine, of the Risen Christ. But on this Sunday, the residents of Kyiv will not be able to go to church because of the government-mandated curfew. ... Because of the threat to their lives. But in that case, the Church will come to the people. Our priests will descend to the underground; they will descend to the bomb shelters. And there they will celebrate the Divine

Liturgy. The Church of Christ brings the Eucharistic Savior to those who are experiencing critical moments in their lives, who need the strength and hope of the Resurrection.

He asked all those who *could* go to church — whether in the still safe parts of the country or abroad — to do so, and to offer their sacrifices for those who could not, especially those under the threat of attack.

"Today, go to Confession," he urged. "Today, receive the Eucharistic Christ, to sacrifice for those who cannot go to church, to sacrifice holy Communion for our soldiers. Today, our life is in their hands. To sacrifice for those who are wounded, for those who are discouraged, for the refugees who are on the roads during this crooked war in Ukraine."

For Sviatoslav Shevchuk and for many Ukrainians, this experience was in many ways nothing new. Anyone over the age of thirty-five or so had at least some dim recollection of what it had been like to live under a Moscow-based regime: to live in the fear that the communist system instilled in a population that had to pretend to support the Soviet Union and Marxism-Leninism — and to be very discreet about their religious Faith.

His Beatitude and many of his fellow Kyivans were now underground, literally. Pastors, he said in the video, would go down to the shelters to celebrate the Divine Liturgy. He had to have been thinking about his own experience as a youth, growing up in a Church that, metaphorically, had been forced underground, and the experience of his parents and grandparents, pastors, and teachers in his underground seminary.

Was history to repeat itself? As bombs fell, reports circulated that once Putin achieved military victory and saw to it that a puppet government was installed in place of the administration of President Volodymyr Zelenskyy, agents would carry out orders to silence Ukrainian political, civic, and religious leaders who could obviously never be expected to support the new Russian-friendly regime. Could there be a replay of 1945, when the Soviet Union went after the leadership of the Ukrainian Greek Catholic Church, imprisoning bishops and priests?

The crisis in 2022 contained parallels to the times of the illegal existence of the Ukrainian Greek Catholic Church. Priests going under-

ground — literally — to serve the Divine Liturgy for a population hud-
dled in dark, makeshift bomb shelters was like the time when priests
went to homes at night and Christians gathered in secret and in silence
to hear the word of God preached to them. His Beatitude's daily video
messages over the internet in 2022 were reminiscent of the Vatican Radio broadcast of the Divine Liturgy into occupied Ukraine in the decades
when Catholics could not go to their own churches.

This book went to press while Putin's war against Ukraine was still
being waged after nearly a year. No one can predict the future. Whatever
happens, Ukraine and the Ukrainian Greek Catholic Church will face
some of the greatest challenges since Soviet times. It is this author's belief
that the experience and wisdom of Sviatoslav Shevchuk — son of proud
Ukrainians who once worshiped underground, a one-time medic in the
Soviet military, a budding theologian who studied in Rome and pastored
in Buenos Aires, and a dynamic Eastern Catholic patriarch who injected
Catholic social teaching into the rebuilding of post-Soviet Ukrainian society — has something to say to those challenges and to the challenges of
the world in the twenty-first century.

2

The Domestic Church

We have seen the true Light,
We have received the heavenly Spirit,
We have found the true Faith,
And we worship the Holy Trinity,
For the Trinity has saved us!

DIVINE LITURGY OF ST. JOHN CHRYSOSTOM

Faithful to Christ's command, priests have for millennia taken bread into their hands and said, "This is my body, which is broken for you, for the remission of sins" — or a similar phrasing, imitating the words of Jesus Christ at the Last Supper. They have taken a chalice of wine and repeated his words, "This is the cup of my blood, the blood of the new and ever-lasting covenant, which is poured out for many, for the remission of sins.

Do this in remembrance of me."

This action has been set in some form of ritual or other, which has come to be called a *Divine Liturgy* or *Mass* or *Holy Qurbana*. It is regarded as the central act of worship in the Christian life. It is the source of spiritual strength for many. The Second Vatican Council referred to the Eucharist as the "source and summit of the Christian life."

But many Christians living under Soviet rule in the latter half of the twentieth century could not receive that Communion, for various reasons. Some could participate in the Divine Liturgy in a spiritual manner, through a radio transmission from the West, as they gathered secretly and listened in quiet in the privacy of their homes. They heard the prayers of consecration — that moment in the liturgy when the words spoken by the priest effected the transubstantiation of the bread and wine into the Body and Blood of Christ. They prayed the hymn quoted at the head of this chapter, expressing the joy of having received Communion.

But, with only a radio in their homes and not a priest, they had not received Christ under the species of consecrated bread and wine but had to make what is called a "spiritual communion," praying that Christ enter into their lives and bring that same grace that they would receive if they were able to stand before a priest, tilt their head back, and allow the priest to drop the Eucharist from a golden spoon into their mouth.

Some Christians were in prison and could not even hear the liturgy in a broadcast. But some of those in prison were priests and bishops. The words of the Master, spoken at the Last Supper, resonated in their hearts: "Do this in memory of me." Striving to be faithful to that summons, they discreetly fashioned bits of scrap metal into liturgical instruments: a spoon to serve as a chalice in which to hold the wine, for example; wine made from smuggled-in raisins, left to soak in water; a few crumbs of bread left over from the daily prison ration. The Eucharist they were able to celebrate from memory provided spiritual sustenance to themselves and other prisoners or inmates in work camps.

The Eucharist is perhaps the most important of the seven sacraments in the Catholic and Orthodox Churches. But in the Soviet Union, other sacraments had to be administered in secret as well: baptism or marriage ceremonies conducted in a private apartment, for example, or confession heard by a priest in street clothes, sitting on a park bench or hidden in a forest.

As His Beatitude Sviatoslav Shevchuk recounts, the Ukrainian Greek Catholic Church might not have existed legally, but it did very much exist in practice. He described how it thrived, for example, in the domestic church, that is, the Catholic family, in the home where he grew up with his parents and grandparents and later, his brother, eleven years his junior.

The practice of the Faith had to be largely a private matter, a fact that could make Catholics feel isolated and alone. But there was one form of technology — primitive by today's standards — that helped ease some of that isolation: the radio, which brought in Vatican Radio. It was a way, Sviatoslav said, for Catholics living east of the Iron Curtain to "live the mystical unity with the Successor of Peter."

Our conversation about this continued:

His Beatitude Sviatoslav: I remember how each word of the Holy Father pronounced and heard on Vatican Radio was followed by those persecuted Catholics. And they were meditating, trying to understand. They very often felt bad. They very often would not be able to follow all those worldwide ecumenical movements, or that openness to the modern world, because we were like a frozen Church, remembering the times before the Second World War as a golden time. But nevertheless, that mystical communion was so evident, and those people were well aware that "we are Catholics, and that is our pope. He is the Vicar of Christ, and he knows about us. He will defend us."

John Burger: You mentioned listening to Vatican Radio at home with your family. Could you describe how Catholics in Ukraine were in touch with the outside world at that time? Was it a case where you had to listen in secret, turning down the radio? Was there material smuggled in that you could read? Were there other ways you could get information? Or was it only things like Vatican Radio and Voice of America?

His Beatitude: Well, of course, listening to Voice of America or BBC was dangerous, so people would listen very secretly, in a low volume.

But Vatican Radio — especially the transmission of the Divine Liturgy — it was an outstanding spiritual event. Often, Ukrainian Greek Catholics would not have a chance to assist at our own celebrations. In some cities of Western Ukraine, the Roman Catholic churches were open, and some people would assist at them. Basically, everything was in Polish, and those people who remembered the conflict between Ukrainians and Poles had some moral difficulties. But very often, even they would overcome those national feelings in order to strengthen their Catholic identity.

But it also depended on the Roman Catholic priest who was assigned to the particular parish. Sometimes he was oriented only toward the Polish community. Some of them were very open to the underground Ukrainian Greek Catholics as well.

But in the circumstances where you did not have free access to your priest, people each Sunday or big feast day would listen to the transmission of the Divine Liturgy through Vatican Radio. And they were praying, kneeling, making a spiritual communion, listening to the homilist.

So basically, Vatican Radio was a way to pray on Sunday, even at home.

In our family, that spiritual moment on Sunday was in secret. We had to close the windows, close the doors, put curtains on the windows, bring the radio into the "upper room" so that the sound wouldn't go out. And we were standing around, like in the church, facing our icons in our house and listening, chanting a little bit.

I remember that they told us on Vatican Radio that if there's no possibility for you to assist at the Sunday liturgy, participating in that celebration through the radio transmission fulfilled your obligation to attend liturgy on Sunday. And we were aware that we were fulfilling our obligation not as a simple external obligation but as our spiritual need. And for me it was very interesting to observe how my grandfather, grandmother, and parents were praying.

What did you notice about that?

Well, there were some very special moments in the liturgical year, especially when we celebrated Christmas and Easter. They were very intense moments. I remember that always before Christmas Eve supper started, we lit candles. We put out the lights and we knelt and prayed together. It was very impressive for me, especially the candle on the table in a dark house. Maybe that prayer, that candle in the dark house, was an image of the existence of the small Christian community in the Soviet reality.

But also, I observed how they would pray by themselves each day. I understood that their relationship with God for them was very important. That was almost the cornerstone of their way of being. And maybe a small kid doesn't understand what they are doing, but he understands very well if they are doing something important or not.

So were all Ukrainian Greek Catholics listening to Vatican Radio like this?

In some villages, people would play their radios very loudly, like a form of protest against the system imposed by the state, because in the 1970s, in many villages of Western Ukraine, Russian Orthodox churches were reopened. So into the closed Greek Catholic churches were assigned Russian Orthodox priests. And they were trying to get people to form Russian Orthodox communities around those reopened churches. Some people would join because it was a chance to publicly and freely pray. But others would say, "No, it's not an authentic Church, because they are Orthodox; they collaborate with the Soviet authorities. And we are *Catholics.*"

And in some villages, it was the subject of arguments, even among simple people. And when the transmission of the Divine Liturgy from the Vatican was broadcast, people would play their radios, even through the windows, in order to protest against those who would enjoy the reopened Orthodox parishes. It was a bit of a polemical gesture — a little provocation.

But I would say that Vatican Radio played a very important role in the spiritual life of orthodox Greek Catholics, those who were willing to maintain their Christian identity. But also, it was a bit of a possibility to receive some objective, authentic information. And for us, it was the possibility to listen to the pope, listen to our priests, to follow some spiritual guidance, listening to the homilist and so on. So the broadcast of the Divine Liturgy was a celebration, but also basic religious education.

So this was in the time of Cardinal Josyf Slipyj, who had spent eighteen years in the Soviet Gulag and spent the rest of his life in exile in Rome.

Yes, it was.

Did you hear his voice in these transmissions?

I don't remember if I heard his voice. But I remember the celebration of the Millennium of Christianity in Ukraine, broadcast from Rome [in 1988]. Cardinal Myroslav Ivan Lubachivsky [Cardinal Slipyj's successor was celebrating. His voice I remember very well. When Cardinal Slipyj died, I was fourteen years old, and maybe at that time it wasn't so easy to understand who is who, whose voice it is.

You describe the situation like worship in the catacombs. What was the danger for you and your family if people heard the sound of Vatican Radio outside your house? On the other hand, some people were blasting the transmission outside their windows. They obviously didn't think it was dangerous.

Well, for some people it was dangerous; for some, not. For example, if you were a simple worker or you lived in the village, or worked on the collective farm, well, nobody would pay too much attention if you are Christian or not. But my mother was a teacher in the music school — she was a musician. My father worked on the railway as an engineer for radio communication. He had special access to some secret protocols, because the railways in the Soviet Union were considered part of the strategic communications. So if they were caught in some sort of religious celebrations, they would lose their work immediately, because if you were working in the educational field in the Soviet Union, and you were not loyal to the official Soviet doctrine, you would be questioned about your ability to educate Soviet citizens. And if you were in an official position and you had access to some secret protocols for the radio communications on the railway, and you were not completely loyal, you could be prosecuted as well.

At that time, there were different policies applied, because in each factory, in each school, in each state organization, there was a special Communist Party group which was vigilant about the doctrinal loyalty of their workers. And in the late 1970s, in the time of Leonid Brezhnev, the credibility of that ideology was highly questioned. I remember — because I studied in Soviet schools — that those teachers who were teaching us communist doctrine, they themselves would not believe in that doctrine. That was very noticeable.

And for me, a small kid, it was very clear that my parents in their Christian belief were authentic. And those who were trying to make Soviet propaganda were not.

I remember my teacher saying, "OK, at home in secret you can celebrate Easter, you can eat Easter eggs. But please don't bring them to school."

So that double morality in the public space was quite evident. That's why, in that period of the history of the Soviet Union, if someone didn't agree with the official guidelines of the Communist Party, you could be prosecuted very severely, but in some circumstances, especially in Western Ukraine, not too much, if you were not active and not trying to organize some plot against the state.

My grandfather — my mother's father — in 1974 visited his oldest brother, who lived in Canada. But it was so difficult for him to get permission to go out of the Soviet Union. I remember interviews that he underwent — in the KGB offices, in the different offices of the state system — in order to get an exit visa. And then, when he came back, wow, so many people were coming to our house, asking how it was there, trying to understand if my grandfather was speaking about the superiority of the capitalist world or not.

You remember that? You were only four years old.

Yes. He came back and shared with us. Each time he would be called to go to an interview with the authorities, we were very scared. And later, when I was seven or eight, I found those forms he was asked to fill out. They were very tricky questions: "Where were you during the Second World War?" If you were present in the occupied territory. "What was your connection or interaction with the Soviet resistance?" He had served in the Polish Army and was a war prisoner in the German concentration camp as a Polish soldier. And we were very afraid that that story would come out, and it was dangerous for him.

Maybe as a small kid I did not focus on what was going on in those interviews, but I remember how our family was scared because of that. Someone said, "Maybe you shouldn't go, just so you're not subject to that additional investigation, because that would be a big exposure for our whole family." Because at that time, just to have relatives outside of Ukraine was considered a disloyalty to the Soviet system. And if you not only get a letter from your brother in Canada but you're willing to visit him, wow, you could be considered a dangerous person.

So it was a whole system of control. But each time those people left our house, my grandfather and grandmother would say, "Oh, he came in order to spy, in order to get information: Are we loyal citizens or not?" I was sitting on a bench listening. When he was put in that situation, my grandfather was forced to hide his authentic feelings. He was always saying, "No, no, here in the Soviet Union we have the best place to live on earth." But when those people left, wow: "God, I saw a real free world. I could not even imagine in the past that something like that existed."

I can imagine how kids like yourself learned from situations like that, that you have to wear two faces — one for the authorities, another for people you trust.

Yes, it was dramatic for me, personally, because for me to change my face was quite impossible. I argued with my grandparents: "Why are you saying things that those people wanted to hear? Why not simply tell the truth?"

Well, we had some arguments, because very often kids or teenagers don't understand the oppressive system of the state or the risks a person can face, or that painful life story of my grandfather and grandmother.

But what I detected [was] when they were authentic and when they were just trying to avoid attention and persecution. Authenticity was something we as kids were able to detect. And I understood that being Christians, being Catholics, was for them something very important, which gave a meaning to their lives.

For example, I was always told that on Sunday, you cannot work. Only foreigners were working on Sunday — only atheists or communists. Even some Russians from Siberia coming to live in our part of Ukraine got used to following that tradition, because if they worked on Sunday, people would laugh at them.

Second, I was also always told that I have to be truthful, especially toward your family, toward those who are truthful with you. So each time I was caught in some small child's lie, I was punished. But not for the punishment itself but to be aware that we cannot lie. "Be truthful — otherwise, we will not confide in you. If you lie, we will not trust you."

Or stealing. In the Soviet Union, it was very common, but in our social group it was strictly prohibited, especially if it was private property. Very often, people would take things home from work, from the factory. But if it was private property, it was strictly prohibited. I remember when I was six or seven years old, and I took a flower from our neighbor's yard and brought it home. My grandmother asked, "Where did you get that?" And I told her.

"Well, now you will go to your neighbor to apologize. You will give it back to him," she said.

Of course, the neighbor was open, smiling and saying, "Good, good, but it's very bad that you would take that. I would give you that flower for free, but you have to ask me."

So it was one way that I was educated. But only afterwards, I understood that all of those traditions and customs were based on the Ten Commandments. So our culture, our way of behaving and living, even in the times of the Soviet Union, was an incarnation of our Christian beliefs. Very often, a teenager might ask, "Why am I supposed to do that? What is the reason?" And the answer was, "There are Ten Commandments, as a rule of happiness, as a way to preserve your dignity and to respect the dignity of your neighbor." It was difficult at that time for us to understand the meaning of the word *love*, but *respect*, yeah, it was very understandable for us. And the culmination of this education was love for God and for neighbor, not because I have to observe the rules but because "I love God, and I will do that because of my respect for you."

That final teaching was imparted to me by the priests of the underground Church.

How did you come to know those priests?

My grandfather — my father's father — was an engineer, a highly educated person. Workers were cutting wood in the forest, and he was the director of a railway station and railroad that was bringing wood from the mountains to the factory. It was difficult for him during the period of the Ukrainian resistance against the Soviet occupation, because the units of Ukrainian soldiers were hiding in the mountains, in the forests. He was an official representative of the government. He had a good job. But almost every day, he would come back from work crossing the field and forest and was constantly encountering those units of the resistance.

Soviets considered railways as a strategic communication. That's why stations and bridges were guarded by military units. You can imagine that man, guarded by the Soviets, walking home, encountering a very different reality on the way. That was the difficulty — to live between two different realities. It was very dangerous as well. He managed to survive only because he had legal work in the Soviet system, but also, he was considered by the local resistance as a part of their community.

Also, he was supposed to be very careful what he talked about because he could easily be denounced to the Soviets, get arrested, and shot, but he could also easily be mistaken as a spy for the Soviets, in that environment of the Ukrainian resistance. To be transparent, to be honest, not to be involved in some sort of espionage, but to be himself was not so easy. To be part of two different worlds which were in an open war was really difficult.

So he had to really convince members of the insurgency that he was not against them, even though he had this Soviet job.

Absolutely. But that was the case for the majority of the civilian population in western Ukraine at that time, because part of the family could be a member of the resistance, and part of the family a member of the "legal society." To work legally, to have Soviet papers, to have the possibility to go to the city, to receive payment, to be a member of that society, they had to be legalized in that system.

You said he was "severely controlled and persecuted." Do you mean he was controlled by his employer?

By everybody, because the Russians invented different ways to control people, so you could never know who you were talking to.

But because he was a professional, the underground Church could be organized around him, and the underground Church was functioning in his house in the city of Broshniv-Osada, where my father was born and grew up. Because my grandfather was legally working, it was secure for the underground Church to meet in his house. His house was considered his private territory, and because of that territory, people felt safe to go there. But when they gathered, they had to close the doors, close the windows, and pray in secret. But because he had a house and had an official job, he could offer a place to the underground priest to celebrate the Divine Liturgy.

My grandfather died before I was born, but years later, it was in that house that I met the underground priest and underground nun for the first time. The nun was an aunt of my father, so she lived on the second floor. It was a small house, and my grandmother lived on the ground floor.

How old were you?

Ten or eleven.

Were you able to attend liturgies in that house?

No. I went when someone died, and my grandmother brought a priest to visit that person's family. It was in the evening. He did not celebrate any Divine Liturgy. The nun told me, "That man is a priest," and I had a chance to talk to him.

Later, when my great-grandfather died, the funeral was at night, in secret. The underground priest would come at night, celebrate Divine Liturgy, pray over the body of the deceased person, and go away.

That was my image of the underground priest — men coming at night. But I saw how appreciated a priest was — how much he meant to the people.

Also, I was a singer, so I was always singing the psalms during those celebrations. So I was invited to enter into the group of seminarians who were preparing to be priests.

When you were listening to the Divine Liturgy broadcast over Vatican Radio, you couldn't actually receive Communion. It was just a broadcast, and there was no priest in your presence to give you the bread and wine of holy Communion. How did you and your parents feel at the time when you would normally go up to the priest, if you were in church, to receive the Body and Blood of Christ?

In the beginning, I did not understand what Communion is at all, because it was not shown by the radio. But I remember, when we started to study English at school, for me it was a very hard subject. I was about thirteen, and my family decided to send me to the English teacher for additional lessons. Each Sunday, I went on foot, walking to another part of the city to attend that tutoring session. And I came back by way of the open Orthodox church. I entered that church, because I had no idea whether it was Catholic or Orthodox. The chants were the same melodies. But I could see those ceremonies, those rites that I heard through the radio. So that music, which I was familiar with, was suddenly visualized.

But didn't you know the Catholic churches were banned and closed, and therefore it must have been Orthodox?

I was thirteen, and I was not quite aware of the formal distinctions between the Orthodox and Catholic traditions. So it was difficult for me to tell the difference.

So you had never been to a Divine Liturgy in person before.

Never. Of course, when you are listening to the radio and you are a small kid without seeing the ceremony, it's very difficult to imagine what's going on there. So I saw for the first time, visibly, that celebration in that Orthodox church. And I remember that in the beginning I was not assisting at the whole celebration. I was just coming, observing, and going home.

But then, I started to ask questions. I asked my grandmother. She was like, "Where did you see that?" and without any hesitation, I said, "Well, passing by, I was just curious — those lights, those smells, that music."

"Aha!" she said. She was happy that I was attracted by that beauty, by that celebration. But she started to more carefully explain who we are. And I remember it was the period when for the first time I received an old book of the catechism of the Catholic Church for children. I don't know how my grandmother got that book. It was published in 1935 or 1936. And she asked me to read that book. There were short stories and questions and answers. Only after, I understood that my grandmother orchestrated that new period of my religious education. I was observing the Orthodox celebration but studying the Catholic catechism.

And I have to say that for the first time, I received holy Communion in that Orthodox church. It was spontaneous, without a good preparation — for which I was blamed afterwards. It was a simple situation, because in the Orthodox Church — and in the Greek Catholic Church today — we would administer Communion even to small children. It was some feast day. Many priests were celebrating. I was standing in front, just looking at them. And when at the moment of Communion priests went out with the chalice, some woman took me saying, "Come, come, come, please." And I received Communion. But I did not understand at that moment what it was. But I went home to my grandma, and she explained to me, "Wow! You know? You received the Body and Blood of Christ. But without preparation. How could that woman do that to you?"

Only afterwards did I understand what happened to me at that moment. It was like, first you receive the sacrament and then you grow in your understanding. Only after, when I entered into the network of the underground Church, did I see the Catholic priests celebrating Divine Liturgy in secret and giving holy Communion. So I had a more conscious, more prepared reception of the Eucharist in the Catholic Church.

Do you remember the name of that church?

Yes, in the Soviet times, it was the open church, the Church of the Dormition. And then that church, with its parish community, returned to the Greek Catholic Church. Today, it's the Cathedral of the Dormition of the Ukrainian Greek Catholic Eparchy of Stryi.

Isn't it normal in Churches of the Byzantine tradition to administer Communion and chrismation (confirmation) to infants when they are baptized? You didn't receive first Communion at that time?

I was baptized in my home. My family invited a priest in secret. He came and he baptized me as an infant. Normally, in those circumstances we would receive baptism and chrismation together, without the Eucharist. It was the rule. And only after, children were prepared in a special way for holy Communion.

But it was different for different groups. Some people would go to the Roman Catholic parishes. But in the Soviet times it was strictly prohibited for the priests to teach catechism to the children. If an underground priest were caught celebrating the sacraments, he would be arrested and then fined. But if he were caught teaching catechism to the children, he would be imprisoned at least for two years, because the Soviet system considered that anti-Soviet propaganda. Priests teaching religion would be considered an agent of the alien ideology, dangerous to the official state ideology. It was an ideological fight.

That's why even Russian Orthodox priests would not teach religion to the children at all. Very often, the only moment of communication of Christian doctrine was the homily. But in each parish a secret agent of the KGB was present, listening to the priest: If he's talking too much or if he's too explicit teaching religion or he's trying to demonstrate superiority of the Christian Faith over the atheistic ideas, he would get in trouble.

So some manifestation of religious life in the Soviet Union was tolerated. It is why some official presence of the Roman Catholic Church was tolerated. Some presence of the Orthodox Church was tolerated. But the Greek Catholic Church was not tolerated at all.

But if anyone tried to spread that religious belief, that was prohibited and would lead to persecution. And those priests who were not just celebrating Divine Office but trying to communicate with the people and be pastors, they would not be tolerated. It's why, very often, people would consider the service of the underground priests to be more authentic because they were not exposed to such control. They were spontaneous. They were, I would say, shorter in their celebrations but more open in their conversations with people.

Very often, underground priests would work in the medical care system because they had the possibility to talk to people without creating suspicion. That's why I have to say that the underground Church maybe in those circumstances was a more pastoral community, and underground priests' pastoral care of the people was more than just administering the sacraments. That administration of the sacraments was always the final goal at the end of a long preparatory conversation. So always, that religious act took place inside of the human relationship, which was not the case in those churches that were publicly tolerated by the state.

3
"Something Will Be Changing"

John Burger: Were you given the name Sviatoslav at birth, or is it a religious name that you took when you became a priest?

His Beatitude Sviatoslav: I have two names. According to the official documents, my name is Sviatoslav. I received that name at birth. But I was baptized with two names: Sviatoslav and Yuri — George — because I was born on the fifth of May, and the sixth of May is the feast of Saint George.[1]

What does Sviatoslav mean, and what has it come to mean for you?

Sviatoslav is a very ancient Slavic name. I was given that name in honor of Sviatoslav the Conqueror, who was a Kyivan prince, the son of Saint Olga and the father of Saint Volodymyr, who baptized Rus' Ukraine.

When I was a child, it was not a common name. Very often, I was

---

1. According to the Byzantine calendar.

teased because of it. It was too long. Some of my friends or teachers tried to give me a nickname, but I fought that: "No, I'm *Sviatoslav*, not Slavko."

But only after, I rediscovered what it means. Sviatoslav is two Slavic words combined: *Sviato* means "something which is holy," and *slav* comes from the word *slavate*, which means "to glorify." So Sviatoslav means someone who glorifies something which is holy. Of course, it is a pre-Christian name,[2] but it reveals some transcendental sensibility of the ancient Slavs.

Later, I learned that there is in the Orthodox Church a Prince Sviatoslav who was beatified, venerated in the city Yur'yev, or Tartuv, Estonia. He's a locally venerated prince-saint, who lived many centuries after.

And Shevchuk? What kind of name is it, and what does it mean?

Shevchuk is a very common surname. It means the son of a shoemaker. In the Eastern part of Ukraine, that profession would have the name Shevchenko.

And of course, the most famous Shevchenko was the nineteenth-century poet Taras Shevchenko, who is considered to be the national bard of Ukraine.

Yes.

Did you live in only one house growing up? What was it like?

Basically, I grew up in the house of my mother's parents. But we rented different apartments in the area. First, we rented an apartment a block away from them, and every day, I went to visit my grandparents, so I basically grew up in that place, which was a private house with a small courtyard.

But then, when I started going to school, my father received an apartment from his job, a little farther away but in the same part of the city. It was an apartment on the fifth floor of a big Soviet-style condominium

---

2. Sviatoslav did not accept Christianity as Volodymyr and Olga did.

building, with only one room. On each floor there were five apartments, and that's how we learned to live in a very close and open community with other families. I had many friends, so it was fun.

Then my father received a bigger apartment in a condominium building of nine floors, just across the street from school, so it was very convenient: From my window, I could hear the school bell. And it was very close to my grandparents' house.

What was the education like in public schools? As you were being formed in the Christian Faith at home, how was the state forming you and your classmates?

The state's policy of education tried to present only their approved heroes, such as the heroes of the pioneer movements, or the heroes of the Second World War, the heroes of the Soviet ideology. They would present you with a personality and explain why you had to be similar to him. But I remember my inner rejection of some of those heroes.

There was a youth named Pavlik Morozov, who was made into a myth by Stalinist propaganda. He was a boy who betrayed his own father, giving him over because of the *kulak* resistance against the collectivization in the Soviet times.

That image of Pavlik Morozov was applied to our own hometown. A boy from Stryi betrayed his own father, who was a member of the Ukrainian resistance against the Soviets, and he was killed by Ukrainian soldiers around 1946 or 1947, because of his betrayal. And Soviet propaganda made that boy a hero — a martyr. He's buried in the cemetery of Stryi.

While that propaganda was trying to glorify someone who betrayed his father, someone who gave up to death his closest family, that image shocked me because my family at that time was everything for me. It was my vision of the world. It was the matrix of my identity. And to betray your father, to give over your family into the hands of the conquerors, was something that made me think that he betrayed himself. It was totally different from what I learned from the religious perspective — loving your father and mother; it was a commandment. It was the first shock for me.

And of course, I obediently had to sit and listen to all those Soviet heroes presented to us as examples of heroic personalities to imitate. I was not openly protesting, but credibility was zero on my part.

You obviously had your own role models: your parents and grandparents, the priests in the underground. Any others?

As a teenager, you look for something authentic and attractive, and I found the underground priests and nuns to be more attractive than those ideologies of the state propaganda. Why? Because that priest or that nun really believed in the word of God that they were preaching or teaching. Even more: They were imprisoned, they suffered, they gave their lives as a witness to what they believed. But those who presented communist heroes did not themselves believe what they were talking about. Even more, they became ideologues of that propaganda because of convenience, because they were well paid; they would have a comfortable life; they would have more privileges and more power over other people.

So if someone did not know the different reality of the life and witness of the underground Church, he would be focused only on this spectrum. But if you have a different witness, a different reality, and you as a teenager have a feeling that *this* is authentic, and *that* is a lie, of course you will be attracted by something that is authentic. That was my experience.

Of course, at such a subtle level, it's not easy to understand where the truth is and where the lie is. But we were observing those who were teaching us, and it's through their reaction or their relation to the subject they were presenting, you would understand or perceive whether they were telling the truth or not. If they themselves did not believe what they were trying to convince us of, what kind of witness could they have?

If the Soviet system was built on lies, did it ever occur to you that it would not last?

I have to say, nobody at that time could even imagine that that system one day could collapse, because it was so powerful, so dangerous, so oppressive. For so many years, the only way to control people was for the system to use violent fear.

But I remember a conversation a small group of people had about the future — a priest, a nun, and some of my relatives. They were saying, "Yeah, there's no hope the system will collapse. There's no hope that one day our Church will be free. Should we continue to go forward on our path as an underground Church or not? What kind of future do we have?"

The nun, who was almost eighty years old, said something that struck me: "Well, you know everything on earth will pass away. And if we here in this earthly life have nothing that would take us to life after death, we'll perish with this life."

That was her reasoning: *We as a Church are giving to that earthly life something that will remain after death. Should we continue? Of course — because it will remain. How? We don't know. But it will remain after death.*

How old were you?

I was thirteen or fourteen. Of course, she understood that those spiritual values, that invisible dimension of the Church, are something that gives us eternal life right now — not only after death — which gives us eternity in the midst of that gray Soviet reality.

But I have to say, I remembered those words when the Soviet system collapsed, because there was something which remained after the death of the Soviet system.

It was a moment when a young boy perhaps was able to think, *Is there something which is forever and something which will pass away, something which is stable, unshakable, and something changeable?* I had never thought about that distinction before.

And after that conversation, I couldn't sleep. I thought, *Well, in what will I have to invest my life? What path to undertake?* And I concluded, *Of course, something which will remain.*

And along with that reasoning, I saw an image — I remember seeing it in some Soviet movie. There was a swamp, and people were trying to find a way to cross it. People were using a stick to try to find solid ground on which to walk. If you missed the path that is solid, you would sink and die. But where is that solid path?

As I say, I remembered that conversation when the Soviet Union collapsed. It was a very difficult time for people, because that which was considered solid, powerful, secure, in one moment disappeared.

In the United States, we considered the USSR the other superpower.

Definitely. Many people committed suicide when it broke up because they lost a lot of money. They lost their life security. For them, there was no future. Even today, some people out of nostalgia would like to reconstruct that superpower in order for them to feel secure in a changing world.

But I saw how the experience of that old nun explained for me the situation in new circumstances.

Going back a few years, you were eight years old when Karol Wojtyła was elected Bishop of Rome. What do you remember of the reaction to the election of this first Slavic pope — a pope from Eastern Europe, from a country that was also dominated by Moscow? Was there some resonance among Catholics in Ukraine?

I was a young boy, so [there were] many things I did not understand. I can remember only some impressions, some emotions.

I remember that situation through the news program on TV. It was every evening at nine o'clock, and it was called *Vremya*, which means "Time." Suddenly, the announcer was saying that, "Today, a Polish bishop was elected as the new pope, John Paul II." And my impression was that saying those words, she was very troubled. From the TV, some sort of fear was transmitted, not just the news.

Well, I was eight years old, so it wasn't possible for me to be thinking analytically. But my impression, on the level of emotion, was that *somehow, they are afraid*. Why?

My grandfather, grandmother, my mom and her sister were present. They were saying, "Something will be changing in the world."

So you would say there was an immediate sense of the significance of this election.

And they argued their reasons: Because if someone from the Soviet, communist part of the world was picked to be the head of the Catholic Church, and they let him go, they are not all-powerful. *Something will be changing.* Nothing more.

So from the TV you could perceive the emotion of fear, and from the audience the emotion of hope.

Were you aware of John Paul's visits to Poland, which are said to have given a great boost to the cause of freedom in that country and led to the fall of communism? And what effect did that have on Ukrainians' aspiration for freedom?

That information was very limited. I understood the importance of those visits, the role of emphasizing the importance of human dignity, the role of Solidarity in Poland, only decades later. We in Ukraine did not receive enough information. There was still a very strong border between the Soviet Union and Poland. At that border, they were trying to stop anything coming from outside: religious information, religious literature, and so on.

Getting back to family life, did you have any tensions with your parents?

I have to say that we did not have any serious tensions. My parents were really caring. My mother was trying to protect me from everything, to prevent any kind of dangers. She was very careful about my health. If I had a temperature, she wouldn't let me go to school, and so on.

So if there were any tensions, it might have been against that overprotection. I was trying to be independent, self-sufficient. And maybe some of my personal interest and participation in the life of the underground Church was in the interest of my personal emancipation from my mother. It gave me a reason to have secrets I could keep from my parents, because I was told not to tell anyone about joining the underground seminary — not even my parents.

Great! I thought to myself. It was a way to become more and more independent.

When I was fifteen, I went to study in a medical school in Boryslav, about twenty-five miles away. I was very proud of myself to be away from my family, to live and study in a different city, because I felt more responsible for myself. But nevertheless, each weekend, I went back home. My father had a car at that time, and he took me back each Sunday evening to the room I was renting in Boryslav.

So it was the first step of my adulthood: You go to study in a different city, you take care of yourself, you face a new situation on your own. But I was so happy at the end of the week to come home, to feel myself again protected by someone.

By this time, you had a little brother.

I was eleven when my little brother, Vsevolod, was born. But at that time, I was the one taking care of him, because my dad and mom were working. I was going to the school in the afternoon. My mom was working in the morning, but in the afternoon, she was back home.

He told me that when he started going to school, you would take him, and his classmates thought he had a "very young father."

Yeah. Maybe it was like an imitation of when I was very young, and my father was taking care of me. Sometimes, I felt myself overprotected, so later, I was in the same way protecting my younger brother. I was taking *him* to school, across the street from our apartment; I was going to the school to bring him back home, and so on. But he was smart enough to present me to his schoolmates because he felt that there was someone who could protect him in case of any fights.

So then you started going to this medical school. Was it a course of studies that would eventually lead to a medical degree?

It was a three-and-a-half-year course that led to a nursing diploma. But it was something more than that. The profession was called *feldscher*.[3] It was like a doctor, but not with a higher education. Such a diploma enabled you to be like a first-aid doctor in rural territories.

But in that institution, we were being trained to be military *feldschers*. In order to be accepted into that school, we had to undergo a very difficult medical exam at the local army recruiting station. The military commissariat had to recognize you as having the health, psychological and physical ability, juridical status, and family situation to be able to fulfill military service. For example, if you were married and had a young family, you could not be recruited into the Soviet Army. If you had health problems, you could not be recruited.

The program allowed you to receive a diploma, and then, after you finished that school, you could enter the university to study to be a doctor. But service in the military was compulsory, and after we graduated, we were recruited into the army. If you excelled in your studies and got a so-called *red diploma*, you had the possibility to avoid military service and go directly to the university. I got a red diploma, but because I was a member of the underground seminary, I was told by my superiors in the seminary, "You have to go to do your military service, because if you're caught in your religious duties without having done military service, you will be sent directly to the army. And if you are sent to the army as an ordained priest, you will probably be killed."

So in order to protect yourself, it was safer to be ordained as an underground priest after finishing military service, because it was the most dangerous period of the life of a young man in Soviet times.

Why would you "probably" be killed?

Because as a priest, you have to pray, even in prison, and you have to fulfill your spiritual duties. And in some circumstances, you can be revealed or caught, and because of that you can be sent into dangerous situations. At the time I was finishing medical school and making my decision, the Soviets were still fighting in Afghanistan. It was a miracle, because I finished my studies in December 1988, and on the 15th of February 1989,

---

3. A word borrowed from German and used to mean medic or non-licensed medical practitioner.

the Soviets started to withdraw troops from Afghanistan.

But if you as a medic are caught as a priest, probably you would be sent to the front lines in Afghanistan. That was the reasoning of the priests in the underground community, not to expose the seminarians too much. I often thought about their reasoning. Often, we wouldn't agree with this, because we were young, and we were willing to put ourselves on the line. Too enthusiastic! But they were very cautious, saying, "Slow down, don't talk too much. Be prudent. You never know who you're talking to. It's not your time yet."

Why did you go to this medical school?

On the one hand, it was a suggestion of my mom. She always dreamed that her son would be a doctor, even though she was a musician. But also, it was an interest of mine, because when I was in school in Stryi, I started to be interested in the medicinal properties of different plants and herbs. I was so interested in the pharmacological substances coming from herbs. Somebody gave me a book about different medical herbs, and I would go into various fields, finding those herbs and so on.

My mom suggested, "Why not do that for a living?"

But also, almost simultaneously, I rediscovered that the medical profession was very positively received in the community of the underground Church. Many priests, even bishops, of the underground Church worked in the healthcare system of the Soviet state. The head of the underground Church, Metropolitan Volodymyr Sterniuk, worked as a *feldscher* in ambulances, until our Church came out from her illegal status.

Even today, I realize that my way of analyzing a situation is a medical one. Very often, I understand a situation in a therapeutic way. But also, it was good for seminary studies, because it was a humanities education.

And we studied Latin.

So the choice made my mom happy, and the superiors of the underground seminary as well.

Was part of your consideration the hope that, even though military service was mandatory, being a medic might help you avoid becoming a combatant?

No. It was helpful. Any profession that could be useful for military service enabled you to have a safe place in the military system. If someone was a medic or driver, he would be able to be more protected from exposure to danger.

But for many reasons, I was urged to apply, even by my family, to that medical school, because it was also a part of the preparation of boys for military service. A big part of Soviet education was pretty much militarized.

And I also received, later on, the approval of Fr. Mykhailo Kosylo, the rector of the underground seminary, because many underground priests and bishops worked as medical assistants. So it was a useful civil profession, even for the future priests of the underground Church.

You were a student in this school when the Chernobyl nuclear power plant had a meltdown in 1986. How much of the news was filtering down to you in Boryslav, which is about four hundred miles to the southwest of Chernobyl?

Boryslav is close to the Carpathian Mountains — a very beautiful city in a green territory. We were fortunate to not be affected directly by the explosion. The radioactive contamination was carried by the wind toward the northwest — toward Russia and Belarus.

Everyone was scared, but the truth of that explosion was revealed many months later, so many people heard about the dangers of increased radiation by listening to the radio stations from abroad — Radio Svoboda, Voice of America, and so on. So from those transmissions, people in Ukraine realized that something had happened. We students at the medical school did not directly participate in the response to that tragedy, but some of our teachers were sent there to help with medical assistance.

Did they come back?

Yes, they did, after a short period of time. We knew that they were among those who were in that zone. They looked very tired, very emotionally exhausted, and they did not share very much about the situation.

They probably saw some horrific effects on the local people.

Probably. Because they went, we knew that something happened, because even physicians and medical professionals were recruited to go there. Why would they be? It meant that there were wounded people there.

But also, we knew that a whole new city was built outside that zone for people who were evacuated. There was interaction among local communities guided by the Communist Party to assist in the building and evacuation and integration of those people who were evacuated.

So there was some sort of forced solidarity, to go there and build that city, to stay there and come back. It was a whole system of how to achieve those requirements of the state for assisting people who were affected by Chernobyl.

Let's go back again to 1978 and consider: From the time Karol Wojtyła was elected to 1989, when the Berlin Wall was breached, that's only eleven years — hardly anything in the greater scheme of things. You spoke of the feeling people had that the Soviet Union was so powerful and would never change, but when we look back now, we realize how much changed over the course of those eleven years. During that decade, were you becoming more and more aware of news from the West, from Europe, from Rome, from the United States? How much did you get from the outside world, and how did it affect people in Ukraine and in the underground Church?

First, I remember when I went to study in Boryslav in 1985, Mikhail Gorbachev was appointed general secretary of the Communist Party of the Soviet Union. From the beginning, we did not realize that something would be changing, because the Soviet Union was pretty strong, and Gorbachev proclaimed some sort of openness of the communist system. That openness was called *glasnost* and *perestroika*, which mean "transparency" and "reconstruction."

The first word, *transparency*, finally manifested itself as a different way to impose the Soviet system on the public. It was like a soft power, rather than violence: *Let's discuss what is true. Let's discuss values.*

So somebody was trying to talk about it. Before, it was very different: *We tell you the story, and you have to receive that story.* But now it was an illusion that somebody is trying to listen to you as well. So it could be some sort of dialogue. Nobody was sure why the dialogue was proposed. *They would listen to me in order to persecute me? To discover my opinion?*

So people were still afraid to openly manifest their opinion.

And *perestroika* — reconstruction — means that we have to review some systems. But we understood that something is bad, that we have to make it better. But to make a statement that something is bad was unthinkable — to say that in the Soviet Union something was bad was a crime. But maybe not so much now.

But what was really for us a change forever, especially the life of the Church, was 1988, the celebration of the Millennium of Christianity in Ukraine. Why? Because for the first time, I heard with my own ears — I still remember the phrase — that Gorbachev, in some high gathering of the Communist Party, recognized the positive impact of religion, saying that religion "concerns some authentic human values."

That struck me profoundly.

At that time, I was still a student in Boryslav, but I understood that the Church would no longer be afraid of this state. It was like the legalization of religious feelings. Nobody can blame you anymore for the fact that you believe in God. They might disrespect you; they might argue with you. But they could not consider your Christian identity a crime in itself.

And I remember, it was the year when Church life started to manifest itself publicly. Different Christian communities were celebrating the Millennium of Christianity in Ukraine.

You refer to the one thousandth anniversary of Prince Volodymyr's deci-sion, in 988, to accept Christianity for himself and the people of Kyivan Rus'. But how could Ukrainian Greek Catholics in 1988 celebrate this if the Church was still underground?

The Orthodox Church celebrated very solemnly, but we were disappoint-ed. Why was the Millennium of Christianity celebrated in Moscow but not in Kyiv? In the underground Church, we always learned that Moscow was evangelized almost two hundred years after [the baptism of Kyivan Rus']. The baptism of Prince Volodymyr happened in Kyiv. So it was a Millennium of Christianity of the Kyivan Church. Moscow at that time did not even exist. So why were they having those celebrations in Mos-cow?

I remember in my city of Stryi seeing a sheet of paper on a telephone pole saying, "The Evangelical community in Stryi will celebrate the Mil-lennium of Christianity in such-and-such a place, at such-and-such a time." I was standing there reading that announcement maybe for ten minutes. *Am I dreaming?* I knew there was a Baptist community in Stryi, because the mother of my grandfather was a Baptist. As a child, I accom-panied her to the gathering place of that community, not far from our house. But it was a persecuted community as well. *Now they were making an announcement on a telephone pole? Impossible!*

And then we heard that one of the underground bishops of the Ukrainian Greek Catholic Church announced publicly that he was com-ing forth out of the illegal status. It was Bishop Pavlo Vasylyk — and he celebrated a public Divine Liturgy in Zarvanytsia, the big Marian sanctu-ary, the national shrine of Ukraine. It was in the forest next to the shrine. It was an outstanding event, with many people in attendance. Police tried to put up an obstacle so people couldn't gather. But the Soviet system was not able to stop that eruption of the manifestation of religious life in different confessions in the public sphere.

I had an impression that the Orthodox Church was trying to absorb inside itself any kind of manifestation of religious life. I remember they had a huge celebration of the Millennium in Lviv, in front of St. George's

Cathedral.[4] I went to that. Patriarch Filaret at that time was Russian Orthodox exarch of the Metropolitan of Kyiv, and he went to Lviv to celebrate that event. But inside that gathering — very solemn, many people, many priests, many bishops — I felt there was something missing. OK, everybody was speaking about one thousand years of Christian life. But there's something missing. And I finally realized what.

Can you imagine a huge celebration, with many priests and bishops, a big crowd and the police not interfering, but when the moment for Communion came, no one was receiving holy Communion? And I thought maybe at that time my thinking was too Catholic.

Why did they organize that liturgy? We as Christians celebrate such events in order to become better Christians. We assist at the Divine Liturgy in order to receive holy Communion. This is the whole purpose of that celebration. Why did you deprive us and those people of the Body and Blood of Christ?

Of course, at home we listened to the transmission through Vatican Radio of a huge celebration of the Millennium of Christianity from Rome, with an outstanding homily from Pope John Paul II, which was not only a remembrance of what happened in the past. The whole meaning of that celebration was to make vibrant those Christian roots, that history, in our own days, to be renewed in our own baptism and to be able to transform a culture, a society in which we live today — because that gesture, that event became a cornerstone of a new era, a new period of history. But with that celebration we can also write a new page in the history of our Church, of our nation. And for me it was the celebration of that Millennium which opened a new page in the history of the Church in that part of the world.

And I think that famous meeting of Gorbachev with John Paul II in 1989 and the official legalization of the Ukrainian Greek Catholic Church allowed by Gorbachev in the Soviet Union was a fruit, a consequence of that celebration of the Millennium. I felt at that time that that very essence, that point which was missing for me in the Orthodox celebration, I found in the celebration of our Church, with the head of

---

4. After the Ukrainian Greek Catholic Church was made illegal in 1946, St. George's was taken over by the Orthodox Church. It was reclaimed by the Ukrainian Greek Catholic Church in 1990.

our Church [Cardinal Myroslav Ivan Lubachivsky], with the Holy Father.

And another feeling that was very important: We were not afraid anymore. People stopped hiding. Priests were celebrating liturgies in public, even if they were still chased by the police, even if there were some tensions between Orthodox communities and Greek Catholic communities. But that new smell: There was no fear anymore. And only afterwards, we realized, if nobody is afraid anymore of that oppressive state, the next step, the next fruit of that revival of Christianity, would be the collapse of the communist system.

That's why we say the legalization of the Ukrainian Greek Catholic Church, as the largest group of social opposition against the Soviet system, was like a pre-annunciation of the fall of the Soviet Union, which happened two years after.

So, listening to Pope John Paul II on Vatican Radio, you had the impression that he was aware of your situation. Did it strike you that he was with you, spiritually?

I'll share with you my emotions and impressions. Some understanding came later.

First, it was an impression of the possibility to compare two different messages which are reaching you. Of course, the celebration of the Millennium of Christianity from Moscow was widely transmitted. We experienced here in Ukraine that there in Moscow they were not talking about us. Everything they were speaking about was *Russia, Russian*, the consequences of [the baptism of Prince Volodymyr] on the Russian State, on the "Russian World." They were speaking about themselves. The consequences of the impression were that it was *their* celebration.

But if you listened to that celebration on Vatican Radio, the message of the Holy Father, he was speaking about us. He was trying to explain what that celebration means for us, what was happening in Kyiv. His message was more understandable for us. Compared to the message coming from Moscow, even though it was coming from Rome, it was *our* celebration. The Russians were speaking about themselves, but the pope was speaking *to* us.

We understand well that the Tradition of the Roman Church is different, that Christianity in Rome started two thousand years ago. But that celebration was something which the Holy Father was trying to bring to the attention of the whole world — what happened and is happening in us, among us. And he came to celebrate *with* us.

So his words were really understandable, really touching us. He was speaking about how I, even here in the Soviet Union, can be a better Christian today because of that celebration.

4
Vocation

John Burger: A person's vocation is a mysterious thing. But can you tell me your "vocation story"? Why priesthood and not medicine or music?

His Beatitude Sviatoslav: Even for me it is not easy to understand. It was not a special pastoral vocation in the underground Church. But maybe a few stories can help shed some light.

First, that story of the conversation of the small group, the priest, the elderly nun: what path to undertake and in what is it really worth it to invest your life. It was a question I grappled with.

Second, I really understood that the underground Church was in great danger, because those priests and nuns we encountered were very old. But they were so important to our people. Who would take their place, when in ten or twenty years they pass away? Who will take the torch from them?

I remember a specific situation when, for the first time, I was praying, saying that I want to be a priest.

At what age?

I was thirteen years old. Along with my father and mother, I visited the Russian Orthodox Monastery in Pochaiv on the feast of Saints Peter and Paul. It was a very exotic place. We decided that since it was a free day — maybe Sunday — we'd take our car and visit. Because of that feast, the miraculous icon of the Mother of God of Pochaiv was brought down, and people were allowed to come and venerate it. I was making a line to approach the icon, and as I was waiting in line I was praying, "Mother of God, I want to be a priest. I know that it's impossible; I know that everybody will say that I'm crazy. But for you nothing is impossible."

It was spontaneous.

"So please, if it is the will of God, if you will do it, I will do it."

Well, with great devotion, I approached the icon and kissed it — with that prayer and expressed desire, with those very naïve words.

From that moment I started to collect information. I began to get interested in Christian doctrines. I started to study the catechism more deeply. You remember that my grandmother gave me that catechism in order to explain the meaning of Communion. And I started to learn more and more, trying to access all kinds of sources for that information.

When I studied in the medical school, the son of an Orthodox priest studied with me. (Now that priest is a Greek Catholic.) I was curious, asking that boy: "Can you ask your father — maybe he has some notebooks from his seminary days." One day, he brought me a notebook on biblical studies. Well, then, I saved up a lot of money from skipping lunch during Lent, and through his father, I bought a Bible. It was all in secret. It was a Bible that Russians had published in preparation for the Millennium of Christianity. It was the only way to get a Bible.

Had you never had a Bible before?

Never.

What about your family?

It was impossible.

I collected money and illegally bought a Bible, and I started to read the Bible with that notebook of his father.

I got more in touch with that system of the underground seminary. My father helped me meet the rector of the seminary in Yaremche, in the Carpathian Mountains, Fr. Mykhailo Kosylo.

So your father was aware of your desire to become a priest.

My parents were aware of my interest, but not too much about my desire. I was told that it is not safe to reveal a desire for the priesthood to the family, only between you and your spiritual director. There were other boys in the seminary, but very often you would not know each other. Your only connection to the network was that priest. If he were caught, the whole network would fail, but if one of the seminarians was a traitor, he could not betray the others because he would not know them.

Your parents knew of your interest but not your desire. What's the difference?

An interest in something is more like a curiosity. We are all curious about new things; there is nothing wrong with that. So my parents were not worried about my mere interest in the priesthood.

However, when an interest becomes a strong desire, it's different — it can have consequences. In that case, my desire for priesthood could be dangerous for my life and that of my family, and that's why I didn't want to share it with my family.

The seminary was not a community; it was not a study program. It was a network of relations. And the way we learned was to receive a notebook, copy that book, and give it back. It was the way to get information, study, reflect, and memorize.

So it wasn't a place where you would all sit in a class and listen to the teacher.

No. I would copy those books at night in the small room I was renting in Boryslav. I had to be sure that the owners of the apartment were asleep, and I covered the glass of the door and the lamp, and I copied the book in complete secrecy.

But can you understand my feeling when the Soviet Union collapsed, and suddenly the way to the priesthood was opened? I remember my prayer to the Mother of Pochaiv: "So, this is your will as well, not only mine." From my subjective point of view, I said, "Well, Holy Mother, in order to open to me the way to the priesthood, you destroyed the Soviet Union. Wow! You are a powerful protector of Christians."

Was your vocation clear to you from an early point, such that it took precedence over marriage? Did you ever date?

Well, about a vocation, I have to say that in different periods of my life I've had different understandings and visions of priesthood as such.

First of all, priesthood is not incompatible with marriage. It is something that always goes together, for us in our Eastern tradition.

But speaking strictly about priesthood, I had never thought that in our Church priests would be somebody to celebrate the divine mysteries in public, someone who would be called to preach publicly, to address his homily to a big crowd, because for us, in that Soviet period, a priest was somebody to come at night, into very small communities, celebrate the sacraments behind closed doors, and leave. So that vision of priest as a service in the parallel reality of the Soviet existence was something very clear in the beginning. ... In the Soviet Union, if someone did not work, he could be prosecuted [for social parasitism]. It was a special word, *tuneyadets* — somebody who eats bread without working. You have to work. You need to have an official job. On the other hand, priestly ministry was something parallel, something more or less hidden.

Also, I never imagined that I would have the possibility to study in the regular, open, and well-organized seminary. And I never imagined that I would have the possibility to study abroad, perhaps to go to Rome, where the broadcast of that Divine Liturgy that we listened to in secret originated. That's why the priesthood was for me a special service to the community, not a clerical position, not as some part of your career. It was your special dedicated service to the community, because our vision of the Church at the time was not a structure but a group of people — basically a community.

Regarding marriage, when I entered that network of the underground seminary, especially that group of Father Kosylo, it was a group of seminarians who were invited to choose celibacy as a state of life for the priesthood. Why? Because in those circumstances, to be a married priest in the underground Church was very dangerous, because you are choosing to be persecuted. Such a choice meant to go against the system. Your choice for priesthood was an act of protest. So being a priest was a danger in itself, and you could not expose your family, your future wife, your children, to that.

But I was a normal boy. Of course, when we were studying in that medical school, we were studying together with the girls — and had good, friendly relations. Always, I was a cantor. Father Kosylo was always looking for boys who are able to chant, to be a cantor in church celebrations. It's how he noticed me: "Wow, that boy can sing!" But also, I was always part of different choirs, and I was a member of the choir of the workers in the petrol industry in Boryslav.[1] And there was a special state organization for exploring and drilling for oil. In the state building for cultural events, they had a special official choir, and I was invited to join, and of course we had a possibility to know a little bit of the local society, local citizens — boys and girls as well. So I grew up with very normal, very open relations with everybody.

But the invitation for the priesthood as a proposal for the celibate life was the predominant thought of my life at that time. Of course, the final decision of my choice for the celibate priesthood I made after my period of Soviet military service,[2] and after I came back from Argentina, where I studied philosophy. So I had a lot of time to discern my vocation before

---

1. A city which has a long history of drilling for oil.

2. After the legalization of the Church.

I made a final decision.

What were some of the books that you read growing up that had an impact on you?

When I was studying in Boryslav, I was renting a room from a Polish family, who basically spoke Polish at home. With them, I had a chance to learn Polish, not only to understand but to read, because they received newspapers from Poland. I started to read Polish detective stories, which were really fun.

But what really changed my life, my imagination, was the book of Henryk Sienkiewicz, *Quo Vadis* — the story of the life of the first Christians in Rome. I read it in the original Polish, and I was really impressed by it. To get a Christian book in the Soviet Union was not easy. I don't even mean a book on theology, but a book like a romantic story based on historical facts.

The next book I really enjoyed was the most famous book of Taras Shevchenko, titled *Kobzar*. My mom gave me a special edition of that book when I was still in school in Stryi. It was a book illustrated with images made by Shevchenko himself, and it was like a poetic reading of the history of Ukraine and Ukrainian culture. The language was so beautiful, and those illustrations as well.

So maybe those two romantic books — Sienkiewicz's *Quo Vadis* and Shevchenko's *Kobzar* — were for me the most important books in that period — fourteen to sixteen years old.

Then I read several other books. It was illegal to read some books on the culture and history of Ukraine and Ukrainian people, because it was a period when such books were taken away from the libraries. But some librarians took those books home, and they were passed around like underground reading.

I remember a small book called *Burning Bush*, a collection of beautiful articles on the most famous Ukrainians. From that book I learned the story of Roxolana, a Ukrainian girl caught and sold as a slave to the Ottoman emperor in Istanbul. She became a wife of the most important Turkish emperor [Suleiman the Magnificent] and played a very important role in the politics of the Ottoman Empire in the second part of the sixteenth century.

And in that book, I learned about the most famous musicians and composers of Ukrainian music, of Church music: Vedel, Berezovsky, and so on. It was like a journey into the cultural history of Ukraine.

Then I started reading historical books, and through that I got interested in the roots of Ukrainian culture and history.

And this is the kind of stuff you would not get in your normal schooling, right?

No, not at all.

While living in Boryslav, were you aware of the Marian apparitions that were taking place in Hrushiv, outside of Drohobych?

Oh yes, of course! Drohobych and Boryslav are near that village. It was 1987 when the Virgin Mary appeared. Huge crowds of people went there. My colleagues and I tried to go there, but we couldn't because at that time we were able to only use public transportation as students. But it was not possible to get there, because of the crowds. We arrived in Drohobych, but from there to Hrushiv we started to walk. But we went through a control point and were stopped by the police. We were afraid of a confrontation with them.

I visited Hrushiv several months later, when this big flow of crowds eased up, but we were told, "Well, the Virgin is not appearing anymore."

But it was something really big, and because so many people were coming to see that vision, it was a big issue for the authorities. They were trying to convince people to stop. They were saying over the radio that there was some sort of illness spreading there. They set up checkpoints to stop people. It was not possible to get into the place by public transportation, so they were putting up obstacles in order to stop people from coming because they were afraid of the massive gathering, because they considered it dangerous for state security.

Once you graduated from the medical school, where were you stationed for your military service?

First, for two months, in a small village called Varpiardka, near Vinnytsya. It was like a military school. Then we were sent to different units throughout the Soviet Union, and I was sent to the military school in Luhansk. It was a school where they prepared the pilots. That's where I spent the rest of my service.

Doing what?

First, I was a member of a special unit of guards. We guarded the aircraft and area of supplies and so on. Later, I was accepted to the medical assistance of the professors and students and pilots.

So you had to be there in case anyone needed medical attention?

No. It was a whole system of medical care for the military. First of all, every time pilots flew, they had to go through a medical evaluation. Also, the whole system of supplies of that military unit: cars and other vehicles. Any time a soldier drove a car, receiving the order to perform his duty, you had to give him a medical certificate that he is not drunk, that his blood pressure is OK, and you had to sign a special list that we called *putyovka*, which enabled that soldier to leave the garage where those military cars for different purposes were kept. I had to testify that that soldier is healthy to drive that car or approach that aircraft.

Also, once a year, each pilot was supposed to undergo a medical survey — even the general overseeing that unit, because as a pilot he was supposed to fly. If he could not because of a health problem, he could not be in that position anymore. That's why the medical assistance to those who were receiving permission to approach the aircraft and vehicles was under medical surveillance. Also, we were offering medical assistance to the soldiers and everyone in that territory because it was an isolated zone, even to the families of those officials who were living and working in that zone.

I assume you dealt with pilots who had been to Afghanistan.

Yes, many of them. Wounded pilots. It's a very traumatic story, that war in Afghanistan.

What was life like for you, someone with a secret priestly vocation, in the military?

It was a very interesting time in my life. I realized that I have something to share with others, because many young soldiers were just disappointed and almost depressed because of the humiliation and disregard for human dignity. In the late 1980s the Soviet Union was already trembling, and the army was not a very well-organized system. It's why inside those military units there were tensions between people from different nations. And I understood that in order to remain yourself, in order to be able to overcome this situation of humiliation, you have to be a Christian.

I started to just share my own religious beliefs with others. Some young soldiers — Russian, Ukrainian, Belarusian — would ask me, "Where do you get that spirit that keeps a joy in you? Why do you not despair?" And I told them, "Because I pray."

"Really? What does it mean?"

"Talk to God," I said.

"And does he really exist?"

And I answered, "Yes, because I exist. He is the source of my life."

At that time, there was a soldier who was not only open to such ideas, but he said, "Well, I would like to become Christian too." And I really regretted that I was not a priest, in order to serve him and administer the sacraments.

5

Grace Building on Nature

John Burger: The way you describe your discernment about whether to be a celibate priest or not reminds me of the story of Karol Wojtyła. He was involved in theater as a member of the underground resistance in Poland, and he had friendships with young women, one of which was quite serious. And he had to choose, in discerning his vocation. Of course, as a Latin Catholic, he didn't have the option to be a married priest, as those in your tradition do. But still, you had to choose. And after the Church became legal again, I suppose it was not as dangerous, so a priest could have a family. How did things evolve with your priestly pursuit after the military service?

His Beatitude Sviatoslav: Well, when I came back from the military service in the spring of 1991, our Church came forth from the underground existence. The head of our Church, Cardinal Myroslav Ivan Lubachivsky, returned from Rome to his episcopal see in the city of Lviv. The illegal seminaries were reopened, including the one in Lviv.

It was actually in a town outside the city, Rudno. So I immediately entered.

Because I had some background with the underground Church, I was sent to study in Argentina, where we have a large Ukrainian community. The eparch of Buenos Aires, Andrés Sapelak, came to our seminary asking for candidates who could join him in Argentina, and he promised to prepare them for the priesthood. He desperately needed missionaries in his eparchy.

So I went to Buenos Aires in August of 1991. It was the first time I went out of the Soviet Union.

There is a substantial Ukrainian immigrant community in Argentina.

Yes. In December, Ukraine proclaimed its independence. On the first of December, there was a referendum on independence, and on the fifth of December, the whole Ukrainian community in Argentina had a big demonstration in the central square of Buenos Aires. We seminarians were carrying a huge Ukrainian flag. It was one of the most powerful experiences. I remember an old woman crying and walking beside me. I asked her, "Madam, what happened? May I help you?" And she showed me her Argentinian papers, which had the place of origin or nationality as "Soviet Union." And she said: "But I'm *Ukrainian.* Imagine, now I can change my document, and it will be written that I am Ukrainian. And I will die as Ukrainian."

I spent three and a half semesters in Buenos Aires studying philosophy in the Salesian Institute. In the beginning of 1993, I went back to Ukraine with a philosophy degree. I could proceed directly to theology in the seminary in Rudno. In 1994, I was ordained a deacon and then a priest.

Argentina must have presented some challenges for you. It was a totally different culture: Hispanic rather than Slavic, free world rather than a closed society where you were closely watched. And studying with the Salesians, you were more in a Latin Catholic milieu rather than a Byzantine one. How did it all work out?

All that adventure in Argentina was on the one hand a very romantic story but on the other very traumatic. Thanks be to God that I underwent that experience after military service, so I was more or less a mature person with a strong experience, as a survivor of the Soviet Army. And in that group of seminarians I was among the oldest, and I was sort of an informal leader of the group.

Second, none of us had any kind of familiarity with a foreign language, and coming to Argentina with its Spanish language was a culture shock. We were very well received by the Ukrainian community in Buenos Aires. At that time, especially, there was a very strong Ukrainian community. Church life was very vibrant. They zealously conserved their Ukrainian origins, and everything was in Ukrainian at that time. So inside that closed community — almost a ghetto in the middle of Buenos Aires — we felt very happy.

But then we were sent to study at the philosophical faculty of the Don Bosco Salesian Center of Studies. And that was a tough experience. I remember entering the big auditorium for the first time and sitting in the front row, right in front of the professor. And for fifty-five minutes, I was paying extreme attention to what he was saying. In fifty-five minutes, I understood two words. It was a lecture on the pre-Socratic philosophers.

When I went out for a break, I was almost depressed. *What am I going to do? How will I be able to understand something, to learn something? And then I have to take an exam — in Spanish.*

My constant prayer was "Please God, help me each day understand at least one or two words more."

But we were listening to those lectures and coming back to the Ukrainian-speaking environment. So probably, if I were to continue in such a system, I would not be able to understand anything. I was really sad, because I was angry with myself. I was angry with God, telling him, "God, why did you bring me here, to a different part of the world? I feel useless. All my life experience is useless. Nobody understands me, and I cannot understand anybody."

Bishop Andriy asked me, "Why are you so sad?" And I spontaneously asked him, "Can you send me to a different community where I don't have the possibility to stay in the Ukrainian seminary but to live in a Spanish-speaking community, perhaps a Salesian one?[1] And he said, "Oh, you want to be a Salesian?" And I said, "Well, I'll try."

So, I was sent to the pre-novitiate of the Salesian community in Buenos Aires, and of course, it was a Latin rite community. We were two seminarians from that group who expressed our desire to try to undertake this path of formation in that Salesian community. And I have to confess that that Salesian pre-novitiate, which we had in the St. Francis de Sales School of Buenos Aires, for me it was a community of consolation in Argentina. Why? Because in that community, I learned Spanish, and at the end of that semester I was able to take philosophy exams, not only oral but written.[2]

So in those six months I made enough progress to be able to follow the lecture, to understand; I had access to the books I needed in order to be well-prepared for those exams, and also that community provided me with very good, adequate human and spiritual formation. We learned about the world that we were inside. I was able to go outside of the closed Ukrainian community to discover Argentina as a society, to discover a wide, vibrant Catholic Church in Argentina, not to be a stranger, but to be well-integrated into that wide community, and also to be able to ask myself, *Who am I as a Ukrainian, as a Byzantine Catholic in that Salesian Latin rite community?*

So for me it was an experience of inculturation, not only to travel to the country but to discover that country, to be able to get in touch with the religious experience, cultural experience, and human experience of the Argentinian society.

So that integration into Argentinian society in the beginning was very painful, but in the end, it was an outstanding richness. And when I finished the curriculum of philosophical study, I decided to ask to come back to Ukraine. But I went back speaking Spanish, having finished a philosophical curriculum of study that no one at that seminary in Lviv had. And my vision of the world and the Catholic Church was very wide.

---

1. Bishop Sapelak was a Salesian.

2. Ninety-nine percent of exams in the Ukrainian Soviet system were oral.

One wouldn't think you'd need Spanish back in Ukraine.

Here's one small way that experience came to benefit me and others: As a special blessing we had a pilgrimage to Lourdes in the summer of 1993 with our rector, an underground bishop, Julian Voronovsky; Fr. John Terlecky, who came from the United States to be our vice rector; and the seminary choir. Father Terlecky was trying to communicate with the authorities, because we wanted to have Divine Liturgy in the grotto, to participate in the procession and so on. And for some reason, he as an American English speaker was unable to communicate with the French priest there.

So suddenly he asked me, "Oh Sviatoslav, you speak Spanish; maybe you can help."

I said, "I'll try." And I went up to that priest and spoke Spanish with him.

We solved all the problems.

You can imagine the bishop, the priests, and the whole group of seminarians looking at me, communicating in Spanish, which nobody understood, and solving the difficult problems that even the vice rector could not resolve.

So at that moment, I was very proud of myself, and I understood. I prayed: "O God, really, I was angry with you. I was asking why you brought me to Argentina. But now I thank you, because at least with that small knowledge of a new language, I was able to offer a special service to my community, to my brothers, to the bishop, to the Ukrainian Church."

What were some of the struggles you encountered on the way to the diaconate and priesthood, and how did you deal with them?

It was a regular seminary life. I would say I always felt lucky being in the seminary, because it was my desire. For many years it was impossible, and we were trying to find any kind of access to theological education and formation. When the Ukrainian Greek Catholic Church came out from the underground and the seminary was open, you had the time and possibility to study and read books that were coming from abroad. I was part of a very big and vibrant community, made up of many different people from different backgrounds and ages. We had boys just out of school; we had older men who were married, with sons and daughters my age. It was a very mixed community, very rich in human experience.

A lot of men came forward to study for the priesthood once the Church was legal again.

It was a community of deep spiritual searching. We were really motivated by our desire to be authentic Christians and to study and know more and deeply about the teaching of the Church and to grow spiritually, because we were aware that we are supposed to not only preach well and be well-educated and attractive for our contemporaries, but also to be spiritual fathers for them.

So we were looking for spiritual guidance, for spiritual fathers. We were lucky to have as a spiritual director at that time [then-Bishop] Lubomyr Husar.[3] He was a superior of the Studite monks, that community which moved from Italy, that famous Studion monastery in Grottaferrata, to Ukraine. Lubomyr was not only the spiritual director, and we had free access to him, but also a professor of ecclesiology.

Also, we had as confessors the heroes of the underground Church — the ones who were many times in prison. I remember a Father Smal, a Redemptorist father. His neck was broken; he couldn't move it because he had been badly beaten by the communists. But he was really a holy man. Also, I remember a very special father, also a Redemptorist, named Father Mykhailiuk, a professor of moral theology but also a confessor, a very illuminated man, a very simple man, sometimes a funny man. But he was always praying. He would walk through the yard of the seminary praying the breviary.

All those heroes of the underground Church are now in heaven. I want to remember them because they were like the stars in my life for that period. We spoke about role models in Soviet times. Those were really heroes which we seminarians would like to imitate in our everyday

---

3. Bishop Lubomyr Husar would go on to become Major Archbishop of the Ukrainian Greek Catholic Church.

life, especially in the choices we're supposed to make in our life.

The third holy man was also a Studite monk, Fr. Vasyl Voronovsky. He was a professor of homiletics, but also an exorcist in the Lviv Archdiocese, and also a confessor. He helped me a lot to understand myself, especially in my immediate preparation for ordination.

That pilgrimage to Lourdes came at a crucial moment to make my life decision: *Will I become a married priest or a celibate priest?* And I was going to Our Lady of Lourdes to ask a special assistance to make the right choice according to the will of God. And Fr. Vasyl Voronovsky was with us as a confessor, and each moment of discernment, I had free access to him, just to be, to talk, and to understand God's will.

So I would say it was a very special period in my life. I have to say that at the time, the seminary in Lviv did not provide a high level of intellectual formation. That's why, when I finished my studies and after my ordination, when I went to Rome and was inscribed into the St. Thomas Aquinas University, many of my grades from the seminary were not recognized. I was forced to repeat some courses or complete some subject which we did not have the possibility to study at all in that seminary. But the human and spiritual formation at that seminary was something more valuable than any kind of other formation you could receive from different communities worldwide. It's why I am so grateful to the Lviv Holy Spirit Seminary to give me that time, to stay there, to discern my vocation, to meet those heroes of the underground Church, and to be well-prepared for ordination.

You said that one of those priests helped you better understand yourself.

That man was Fr. Vasyl Voronovsky. Very often, it is difficult to understand: *Is this my vocation or simply my desire? Is it the will of God or my imagination? How can I discern?* He helped me a lot by saying, "Well, do you really need this, or is this simply your desire or expectation? Can you live without it or not? Is it something that is a part of your fantasy, or is it reality?"

Of course, it was an issue to examine the depth and how serious some relationships were. Of course, I had to examine my relationships with the girls. I was in a good friendship with a girl, but I had to understand, was it a serious relationship, to go forward, or was it like you have to be as others are, simply imitating the behavior of others? Are you looking for girls because everybody is looking for a wife before ordination? Or is it something without which you cannot live?

When you talk about "looking for a wife before ordination," I wonder if sometimes seminarians feel pressure to find a bride quickly, before ordination. That might lead to an unhealthy approach to marriage, no?

Yeah, not only are you trying to stick to a schedule, but also you are under the pressure of the environment, because, well, that group of persons is preparing for the married priesthood, and you have to be married in order to join that group. Or secondly, you have to marry during this next six months, before ordination to the diaconate. But are you ready? And many boys were making choices without a very mature human relationship with their future wife. And they lived some very difficult moments in their married life later.

That's why it was so important to have someone help you, first of all, to understand yourself, not to be a victim of the pressure of some stereotype, to understand your own character, to examine the human relations which you are living at the moment, and in the middle of that to find the will of God.

It was very interesting, because it was a totally different situation from what I was discovering about the vocation to the priesthood five years earlier, when I was a member of that network of underground seminarians led by Father Kosylo. After the legalization of our Church, you were no longer forced to choose the celibate life. But in those circumstances, I remembered that first love, that first feeling and first discovery of a vocation to the priesthood in this earlier period of life.

And I was also very grateful to God to have had the possibility to discern that vocation inside different circumstances — studying in medical school in the Soviet times, living that inner desire while in the Soviet Army, then studying in Argentina and coming back to the Lviv Holy Spirit Seminary in Rudno. I was the same person with the same vocation, but God was good enough to test me in the different situations, with different external circumstances. But finally, I could understand who I am and for what kind of service, what kind of vocation, I was called.

Cardinal Lubachivsky ordained you a priest on June 26, 1994, and you went on to do studies in Rome later that year. What led you to do a doctorate in moral theology?

To study in Rome was not my decision but the decision of Cardinal Lubachivsky, because at that time we had a huge number of young seminarians who were willing to become priests. Our Church at that time had a very big shortage of priests, but we had very few professors who were able to provide an adequate intellectual formation. … I was a young, celibate priest, which is not so common in Ukraine. I was the one who had the experience of studying abroad.

I remember the audience with Cardinal Lubachivsky. He told me explicitly: "Well, you speak Spanish, so for you it will be a lot easier to learn Italian. We desperately need someone who can be a professor in our seminary. And you have an interest in studies. So please, go study something that is most attractive to you and most needed by our people."

And the whole issue of morality, moral theology, at that time was an urgent need, because the issue of moral dualism in the post-Soviet society was a big problem. People very often were divided inside. You never knew if you were talking to the right side of the personality.

A number of priests returned to the Catholic Church from the Orthodox Church, and many never had any kind of training in Catholic moral studies, especially on family issues. We studied moral theology according to ancient books in the seminary in Ukraine. That Redemptorist Father Mykhailiuk was teaching moral theology from a book translated from Latin during the time of the persecuted Church.

So, according to those needs and along the lines of my personal interest, I went to St. Thomas Aquinas University to study moral theology. I was well-received, but when the dean of the theological faculty examined my curriculum of studies, he asked me for one year to complete my studies in theology. All my curriculum of philosophical studies from Argentina were recognized, but the theological studies were not enough in order to start immediately on licentiate studies for moral theology.

So for one year I was following a specially established program of theological studies to complete my curriculum. Only after that did I enter the so-called second cycle of theology — the specialization in moral theology. Because I made good progress, I had good marks, and my progress was evaluated as very positive, I achieved the licentiate of sacred theology (STL). I wrote a thesis, I passed my exams, and I was able to start immediately on the doctoral studies.

You wrote your doctoral dissertation about Paul Evdokimov (1902–1970). Tell me about him and why you chose that topic.

Whenever I lived abroad, beginning with my experience in Argentina, I was forced to interpret: *Who am I, and why am I a Byzantine Catholic in a Latin Catholic environment? Why am I making the Sign of the Cross from right to left, and what does it mean to be a Byzantine Catholic?*

Paul Evdokimov was a Russian Orthodox theologian, a lay person, who did the same thing during his life in France, trying to explain in the period of the Second Vatican Council what the Orthodox spirituality, liturgy, and theology is all about to a modern audience. So his specific attractiveness was that freshness of the Eastern spirituality, the theology of the Fathers of the Church, reinterpreted in a way to be understandable for modern culture. And I found his theology very understandable, providing answers for my personal spiritual search, because when I was studying theology, I was not trying to memorize some theories or to comprehend some abstract way of thinking. I was trying to meet God, understand him, through the spiritual and doctrinal tradition of the Church. So basically, those theologians who helped me understand better my own personal spiritual questioning were very attractive for me.

The first book I read by Evdokimov was translated into Polish, *Woman and the Salvation of the World.* In this book, Evdokimov was trying to explain Eastern Christian anthropology, making a parallel with the psychological research of Carl Jung. And I found that kind of dialogue between tradition and the modern world, Christian anthropology and new anthropology which was formed by psychological researchers, very interesting. So I was really impacted by that book.

I started to read another of his books, at the very beginning of my studies in Rome, and when I finished that first year of my theological preparation and entered into the licentiate studies, I was looking for the subject of my research and the subject of my diploma thesis. My advisor was a professor of anthropology, a Dominican from Colombia, who had never heard of Evdokimov. He did not understand very well who we are as Byzantine Catholics. But when I explained to him the way to understand the human being according to the patristic tradition of the Byzantine Fathers of the Church, he was fascinated and said, "Well, you can take up that subject."

How did you explain that to him?

The theology of St. Thomas Aquinas is based on some philosophical arguments of Aristotle. The discussion was about what human nature is all about. What is natural, supernatural, preternatural for the human being? Such a distinction in Eastern anthropology does not exist. Because basically, human nature is defined in this vision as nature *after* original sin. What is natural today for man? Of course, grace is *super*natural, something beyond the simple human nature.

But according to the patristic tradition, the notion of human nature is connected not with original sin but with the original creation of man. The natural will be for the human being everything that is before original sin. This is why the whole theological system of the theology of grace would be shaped in a different manner in the Byzantine tradition, and the creation of man in the image and likeness of God will define human nature. So this is why the Byzantine Fathers would say that divine grace for a man is a part of his nature, is a natural environment in which the human being can grow, develop, flourish, and be [himself]. So, without divine grace and without the presence of the Holy Spirit, there is no anthropology. That's why the whole anthropological discourse is a theology for the Byzantine tradition.

That professor was just fascinated, saying, "Well, that is something very familiar even for us, because yes, we do make some distinction between natural and supernatural, but even according to Aquinas, in order to achieve virtues, in order to be yourself, you have to live with divine grace. That grace is necessary to heal the wounds, to elevate human nature into the maximum realization of the human potential. So there isn't any opposition between nature and divine grace. Indeed, *gratia supponit naturae*. Grace needs a nature to rely on, and human nature, even after original sin, requires healing acts of divine grace. Divine grace, even in the Thomistic tradition, would be understood through the effects of divine grace in the human being. *Gratia sanante, gratia sanctificante*, and so on."

So there is no contradiction between the Western and Eastern anthropology, and indeed, there is harmony, and those two perspectives need one another. Because without the Western tradition, the Eastern perspective is too spiritual, mystical, not concrete and real for everyday life. And for the Western perspective, it is important to have this mystical orientation [so] we can understand ourselves through that perspective of the final goal, final vocation.

The title of my licentiate diploma thesis was "A Concept of Personhood according to the Theology of Paul Evdokimov." My professor told me that the whole concept of personhood could be a meeting point of different perspectives, different fields of human knowledge, moral theology, anthropology, juridical studies, social studies, and all other humanitarian studies of the modern world. "But you will study that concept according to the theology of Paul Evdokimov." And also, his invitation was to realize from which sources Evdokimov is taking his ideas and to figure out if he reinterprets correctly the theology of those Fathers of the Church from whom he is taking that theological material.

So my licentiate thesis was the first chapter of the bigger doctoral research, which I did two years later. And the title of my doctoral research was "The Life Transfigured in Christ: The Perspective from the Theology of Paul Evdokimov," because my next professor, who helped me to take a second step in my research, was trying to help me undertake the following methodology: OK, here you have Evdokimov, in his way to interpret your tradition, the Byzantine spirituality and theology. Very good. He's a good theologian. You started to detect his sources. Very good. So we can find the second point, but then we have to make a line and suggest how that kind of thinking, that kind of interpreting the Church tradition, moral theology, the foundation for moral theology, can help us today to solve our problems.

So we can make those two points, and from them draw a line toward the biggest questions of theology of our day. That's why the subtitle is "The Perspective *from* the Theology of Paul Evdokimov."

After graduate school, even as a priest, you spent a lot of time as an educator or administrator. And now you've been a bishop since 2009. All that seems quite far from what you originally imagined priestly life to be.

I was the first theologian with a doctoral degree who, after the legalization of our Church, came back home with that title, as a professor and educator. It was 1999. At that time, the auxiliary bishop of Cardinal Lubachivsky was Lubomyr Husar. He knew me very well from when he was one of our spiritual fathers in the seminary in Rudno. He visited me very often while I was studying in Rome, and when I finished my doctoral studies, he asked me to come back home, and he directed me to the Holy Spirit Seminary.[4] I started to teach theological anthropology and moral theology, the two subjects in which I was a specialist. I was also vice rector of the seminary. I was not only a teacher but also a formator for seminarians. It was the second big challenge for me, to be an educator and formator for a huge number of seminarians. At that time, we had 250 seminarians, and we were nine priests in that seminary. So it was a big challenge.

What about parish work?

Since I was ordained, I have always considered priesthood my primary vocation. So I was trying always to be engaged in pastoral ministry. While I was studying in Rome, we were assisting Ukrainian migrants

---

4. By this time in Lviv.

coming to Italy in massive numbers. I lived at the Ukrainian Catholic parish in Rome, Saints Sergius and Bacchus in Piazza Madonna dei Monti. At that parish, I was basically fulfilling the duties of the vicar, and we were assisting those people in difficult situations, finding themselves at the beginning of their journey in Italy. I lived at that parish for five years. I was studying, yes, but also I was offering pastoral care.

Also, in 1997, His Grace Lubomyr Husar asked me to start organizing a parish community for Ukrainians in Greece. It was in the beginning not systematic pastoral assistance, but I was going several times a year, especially for the big feasts, like Easter or Christmas. I was always spending two or three weeks in Athens, and basically, I was the one who lay the first foundation for the Ukrainian parish there, received by the Exarchate for the Byzantine Catholics in Greece. We were hosted by Bishop Anargyros Printezis at his Cathedral of the Holy Trinity in Athens. He offered not only his church but also his residence for the Ukrainian community. And I organized the parish, a school for the children, and so on. It was my first parish experience, to organize a community in a new country, to gather people who were spread around that country, to offer them a place to stay and spiritual care from the very beginning.

Sounds like a lot of work.

Yes. I came home in 1999 through Greece. I defended my doctoral thesis in June, and from Rome I went to Athens. I spent three months with that community, also studying modern Greek at the philosophical faculty of Athens State University. And only in the beginning of September, when classes were supposed to start, I left Greece for Lviv.

But even when I was teaching in the seminary, for several years, I was still taking care of that community, going back to Greece for the big feasts, to assist those people. So it was my first parish, and my first love.

6

Transformation

John Burger: Pope John Paul II visited Ukraine in 2001. Were you involved in preparing for his visit?

His Beatitude Sviatoslav: Not directly. Fr. Bohdan Prach[1] was the key person of the committee that prepared for the visit. But he was at that time rector of Lviv Holy Spirit Seminary, so while he was working on the papal visit, I as vice rector was very much engaged in guiding the seminary. So my service for the papal visit was inside the seminary community in order to allow others to be active outside.

But as a seminary we were very involved in the preparation of this huge space where the celebration would take place, to build, to prepare the altar, and [to] organize the celebration. During the pope's visit to Lviv, the whole seminary was involved, because there were so many duties that we were supposed to complete. I was one of three masters of ceremony for the Byzantine Divine Liturgy at which the pope presided.

---

1. As of this writing, Fr. Bohdan Prach was rector of the Ukrainian Catholic University in Lviv.

It was really a historic event: Almost a million people gathered. And we were supposed to provide for them the possibility to receive Communion. And it was the liturgy during which the new Ukrainian martyrs were beatified.

There was also a huge group of journalists from around the world. During the Divine Liturgy, Fr. Ken Nowakowski[2] was taking care of this group of journalists. And he asked me to respond to a phone call from a journalist from Mexico: "Talk to him in Spanish and explain what is going on here." For me, it was a very touching moment, because standing behind the scene, with this loud, solemn choir singing, with the presence of the Holy Father, I was talking to this journalist from Mexico, trying to explain to him in Spanish what is going on — in a very concise way.

But I think that it was historic. It was the glory of the resurrected Church, but also a crucial impact on Ukrainian society. So many simple people were saying, "When the pope touched Ukrainian soil, communism will not come back again." So, for the people who suffered the persecutions, who knew personally those martyrs who were beatified that day, that visit meant the end of the whole history of communist oppression in Ukraine and the beginning of a new era.

And what a difference between this event, where you and your confreres were responsible to make sure that everyone in this million-person congregation could receive Communion, and that Orthodox liturgy in Lviv you described earlier, during the celebrations of 1988, when Communion was not offered to the faithful.

Absolutely. So it was an *Event*, with a capital *E*, which marked a new period of the history of Ukraine.

Lubomyr Husar became a bishop in 1995 and Major Archbishop of the Ukrainian Greek Catholic Church in 2001, and then a cardinal. In 2002, you became his personal secretary. Tell me about working with him.

---

2. As of this writing, Bishop Kenneth A. Nowakowski was eparch of the Ukrainian Greek Catholic Eparchy of the Holy Family in London, England.

I have to say that I was really surprised that he again remembered me and asked me to help him as his secretary, but also as an administrator of his curia in Lviv. He started to develop his curia because he was fulfilling several duties at the same time. He was the bishop of the Lviv Archdiocese, which is a big territory. So every two months, he called our bishops throughout Ukraine to the Synod. But also, he was head of the worldwide Ukrainian Catholic Church. So in order to be able to fulfill all those levels of service, he had to have well-articulated structures. To be his secretary meant not only to open his letters, to prepare a schedule for audiences, and to prepare programs for his visits. It was first of all a discernment about to which level we are supposed to move, and to help him delegate his competence to the various Church structures.

It was a very interesting service, because working with him I was rediscovering my own Church. My cooperation with him started with some small service for him to help work with Spanish-speaking correspondents. I remember that in 2002, Lubomyr sent me for the first time to Spain, to a conference on bioethics, but also to study the pastoral needs of Ukrainian migrants in Spain. I went there, met with our people, with the Church authorities. I brought to him the contacts. But then, you have to maintain and develop those contacts, write letters, be in touch with different bishops, prepare adequate candidates for priestly ministry in Spain. It was part of my duty to take care of the Spanish-speaking world and Spanish correspondents. I used to go once a week to visit Cardinal Husar and work on that correspondence and listen to him and write letters back and so on.

But one day, suddenly, he asked me to be his secretary and to become an administrator of his curia, which is much more work. So it's impossible to come once a week and do all that stuff, especially since at that time I was vice rector of the seminary. I was teaching in seminary and the Catholic University. I was vice dean of the philosophical and theological faculty, and chair of the theological department of the Catholic University. And now that duty of secretary of the head of the Church? How can I survive?

He asked me to remain vice rector of the seminary, maybe leave some duties in the university, keep my responsibilities as a professor and theologian, but at least three days a week come to assist him in his curia as his secretary. So I was moving between three different institutions: seminary, Catholic University, Patriarchal Curia. That was my work. I was almost exhausted.

But the most challenging and difficult period of my life was the Orange Revolution at the end of 2004. It was a very shaky period in Ukraine. After the open fraud in the elections of 2004, people were going into the streets protesting the falsification of the elections. And our Church was always a voice of truth and a very important moral authority for society. And of course, the responsibility of the spiritual guide of our Church was so important. I was blessed to be with Lubomyr Husar at that time and to see him, how he was guiding the Church and how he was delivering a very profound spiritual but also clear social message to society.

Tell me more about that.

He was focused on explaining what it means to be a free man, what freedom is all about, and he always spoke about dignity and responsibility. He posed many different questions and delivered various messages at that time. But one struck me. When journalists asked him, "Who are those people standing in the middle of the city? Are they a dangerous crowd that we as a society, as a state, are supposed to defend ourselves from?"

And he responded: "They are responsible citizens, and they are demanding authentic results of the elections. They are defending their votes, because they are convinced that the results of the election were manipulated, and the correct results were not revealed."

So who are they? "Responsible citizens." For the post-Soviet context, such an answer was a small mental revolution, because not only politicians have responsibility, but each citizen has to be responsible, to defend his own rights, his own vote, and that responsible citizenship is a source of hope for the future transformation of our country. The personal responsibility of the citizens, their own vote, is a source of hope for the future transformation of our country. The personal responsibility of the citizens will make our country free. It was like a message destroying the whole ideology of the paternalism of the state or of the political system, that someone else will take care of my future and take care of me; someone else is supposed to be responsible for freedom, for the European standard in my country. But Lubomyr Husar pointed out the personal responsibility of each citizen of Ukraine.

What was at issue in the Orange Revolution?

The Orange Revolution was a protest against the falsification of the election in which Viktor Yanukovych was trying to get elected president. His opponent was Viktor Yushchenko, who was considered the pro-European, pro-Western candidate. And the result of that protest was that the Supreme Court of Ukraine sanctioned a third round of voting. Because of such a protest, so much evidence of falsification was brought to the court, and the court started to consider that evidence. And because it was more than enough to make clear the massive falsification of the results, the Supreme Court declared the result invalid and decreed that the election be repeated. And in that third round, Yushchenko was elected.

It sounds like Cardinal Husar was a very public figure at the time.

I would say he was the most important public person as a moral authority for Ukrainian society at that time. People were protesting in the city of Lviv. Our bishops were gathered in their synod in the metropolitan palace, and from the closed windows we could hear the crowd shouting: "Yushchenko! Yushchenko!" And our bishops were supposed to make a statement about the situation. I was preparing materials for them.

Finally, the bishops agreed on the text of the statement and delivered a press conference immediately after the synod was ended. I was the one to mediate. One of the journalists asked Cardinal Husar, "What should people do if the president gave an order to shoot protesters on the street?"

Everyone was silent, waiting to hear what Husar would say.

"Well, I cannot even *imagine* the president would *ever* give such an order," he said.

So, just by the way he said it, he declared such behavior criminal.

Right after the press conference, I approached him, asking: "Your Beatitude, I want your blessing, because this evening, I will leave with a whole busload of seminarians to take part in the protests in Kyiv." And he blessed me, solemnly. And with that statement of the bishops, that evening, with forty seminarians, we left for Kyiv. We were driving all night, and in the morning, in cassocks, we were with the protesters in the middle of the city. I was the first priest to publicly celebrate Divine Liturgy in the protesters' camp, in the middle of Maidan Square. And I read the statement of our bishops. People were crying, applauding, saying, "Thank you. At least someone told the truth."

How could the Church take a stand without being political?

It was very tricky, very delicate. Our Church was not taking the side of any candidate but stood up defending authentic democracy against falsification. The authentic will of the people has to be respected. That was the most important statement. It was a very dangerous situation because everybody knew that Moscow was trying to interfere in those elections, to impose Yanukovych. In fact, he was elected president five years later.

But it was a delicate moment. Thanks be to God, it was resolved without violence, because of the position of the Church. The Church was not trying to take one side or the other, because *that* would provoke violence. But the Church was defending the authenticity of the decision of the people in the elections. Nobody could say that was direct interference into politics. It was moral standards, fostering the post-Soviet society which was trying to learn how to build the political system of our country in a democratic way.

You became rector of Holy Spirit Seminary in Lviv in 2007, but the following year, your life would change drastically.

It was the feast of Saint Nicholas in 2008. It was an ordinary day, but Husar was recovering in the Sheptytsky Hospital near St. George Cathedral in Lviv. He called and asked me to visit. "I want to talk to you."

I went, and he told me, "The Holy Father [Pope] Benedict blessed the decision of our Synod to appoint you as a bishop of the Ukrainians in Argentina."

I was shocked, because suddenly, I realized that everything I was doing until then, I had to leave. Always, I understood that my Church wanted me to be a teacher, a theologian, a formator of new priests. There were not too many theologians in the Catholic University at all. The university was trying to receive an ordinary accreditation from the Congregation for Catholic Education in Rome. So each doctoral diploma in theology was so valuable for that period, and I was among the few persons having that qualification.

But my answer was, "Your Grace, if you are saying the Church needs me there, and that is the will of God, I'll accept it." Not because I was looking for any honors in Argentina. I have to say that for many people, my assignment to such a mission in Argentina looked like a punishment: *For some reason, they sent him away from Ukraine.*

When you served in Buenos Aires, were you the eparch or an auxiliary bishop or what?

All the time I studied in Rome and then worked in Lviv, I maintained my relations with the people in Argentina. And I knew the situation there very well. So our eparchy in Argentina was desperately in need of a new hope, a new leader, because that huge community was falling apart because of the lack of priests, because the bishop was old and sick; he was not able to fulfill all his duties, because it's such a big country. The year before, our Permanent Synod visited Argentina, listening to the people.

I was assigned as an auxiliary bishop of the Ukrainian Eparchy in Argentina. But six months after my arrival, my ordinary bishop presented his resignation.[3]

So, I was ordained a bishop on the seventh of April, 2009. I moved to Argentina after the school year finished, in the beginning of June. And in October of the same year, Bishop Mykhailo Mykycej presented his resignation, which in one month was accepted. And Pope Benedict appointed

---

3. Because he reached the mandatory retirement age.

me as administrator of the eparchy, because in order to be an ordinary bishop you have to be a citizen of Argentina. And I was inclined to receive citizenship, but as long as I wasn't a citizen, I was able to be only an administrator.

And Jorge Mario Bergoglio, as archbishop of Buenos Aires [1998–2013], was my direct superior and president of the bishops' conference, the one to whom I was directly related in that situation.

How can that be, if he was the archbishop of the Latin Catholic Archdiocese of Buenos Aires? Wouldn't your direct superior have been Cardinal Husar, as head of your Church?

The problem is, there is a special way to assist the Eastern Catholic eparchies in the countries where there is no metropolis for that Church. You cannot be just disseminated in the world structure as an eparchy. You have to be included into the broader Church body. And because we didn't have a metropolis in Argentina, I was a suffragan of the Archbishop of Buenos Aires, and the Archbishop of Buenos Aires was the ordinary for the Eastern Catholics in Argentina, who did not have their own ecclesial structure.[4]

Of course, as a bishop of the Ukrainian Greek Catholic Church, I was a member of the Synod of the Church. The synod is the Church body that has the right and duty to elect new bishops for that see, presenting the candidates of its election to the Holy Father. But in the ordinary life, the bishop of the Ukrainian eparchy in Argentina is subject to that metropolitan structure of the Buenos Aires Archdiocese of the Roman Catholic Church. And he is also a member of the bishops' conference in that country. I was introduced to that conference by Cardinal Bergoglio.

What do you remember about that moment?

I was thirty-eight, and I remember those very solemn-looking bishops turning their heads toward me and asking, "Well, who's that altar boy? Did he receive his first Communion yet?"

---

4. That included Melkites, Maronites, Russian Catholics, Romanian Catholics, and Armenian Catholics.

But seriously, I have to say that the bishops in Argentina were very open and very kind to me, and Cardinal Bergoglio himself was to me a good father. I had no idea what it means to be an Eastern Catholic bishop in Latin American culture, and I have to say that really a project of my life was to be a good bishop, a good pastor for my people in Argentina. I remember having some talks with Cardinal Bergoglio, and he taught me that being a bishop in today's world, especially in Argentina, no longer means to be distant [from people] and a prince of the Church, but to be a humble servant and friend of the poor.

So I had to rethink all liturgical questions, all pastoral issues, in order to be effective pastorally, a bishop for the Ukrainians who were spread throughout Argentina, a country ... bigger than Ukraine. And in that country, I had only sixteen priests. So very often, in one parish, where there was an old priest, I was supposed to come personally, to be a pastor to those people.

In what ways was Cardinal Bergoglio a father to you?

When I went to Argentina as a bishop, I have to say that I had no idea what it means to be a Ukrainian Catholic bishop in that country at that moment, because of the political situation in Argentina, because of the social challenges, because of the life of the Church. My question was, "What does it mean to be an Eastern Catholic in the Latin American culture?" And as a bishop, I was a subject of the not-so-easy-to-understand juridical system of Argentina. *How can I move inside of that situation?*

So, Jorge Mario Bergoglio was the one who took me by the hand and introduced me, not only to the gathering of the bishops but to the reality in Argentina. He taught me what it means to be a bishop in Argentina, that the bishop is not an emperor or a pharaoh sitting on the throne. The bishop is a servant.

Would you say he taught by word or example?

By attitude, because he was trying to help me understand what kind of behavior I have to adopt in order to be efficient, how to present myself to the priests and to the people, because for me it wasn't easy to win the confidence of the priests and laity, as I was a stranger. He was the one who was interpreting some difficult situations for me in order to explain how I can solve those situations.

What situations?

For example, my predecessor in Argentina accepted twenty-six Ukrainian immigrant families after the fall of the Soviet Union, and those new im-migrants lived in the bishop's residence and around the cathedral. I found a very strange situation, and Jorge Mario Bergoglio explained to me that if I did not try to put some order into that situation, our eparchy could lose that property, because if those people presented to the state evidence that they lived there for a certain period of time, that property could be-come theirs. And I started a juridical process asking the court for justice — not to throw those people out onto the street but to put order into the situation, to claim the right of the owner.

But it was not easy to understand what I had to do. I had to find the right lawyer to assist me as a bishop. I had to help those people — be-cause they are my parishioners — but on the other hand I had to bring order into the situation.

Twenty-six families. All those people living in the bishop's residence?

It was not just one building; it was a territory. There were several locations around the cathedral. In Argentina, space is abundant, and there's the pos-sibility to stay outside the building. It's a different culture. In Ukraine, we're always hiding inside the building; we expand spaces inside the building. But in Argentina, it's different: small rooms, but big courtyards.

Were there other examples of how Cardinal Bergoglio was a father to you?

I had several very important conversations with him. Especially in East-ern Europe today, the image of the bishop — his status, his role — is very much linked with the past. The Church in Eastern Europe — not only

Catholic but also Orthodox — would remember the Church's status in the state before communism, and subconsciously, Church leaders would consider that a golden time in the Church. And very often, after the fall of communism, they had temptations to restore the glory of the Church they lost because of communism, to restore the kingdom before communism.

Why do I call this a temptation? Because in that vision, we are restoring the past; we are going back, not forward. We are claiming something which nobody today can provide for us. We are in the illusion of the Christian state, which will treat a Church as one of the pillars of that state, which is no longer the case.

And what is the image of the bishop in this vision? It's a prince — a prince who, with a mentor's tone, tells others what they should do, a prince who expects everyone around him to venerate him, not because of what he's doing, what kind of person he is, but because of his status.

That is the whole temptation, and I think many bishops today, at least in our Church, realize that we cannot be a bishop-prince today; we have to be a bishop-servant. We cannot claim our status in the state; we have to serve in that state to be authentically human. We cannot give orders to the people what they should do; we have to preach the Gospel. We cannot use coercion or force to impose a Christian Faith, but we have to be witnesses and propose in a very attractive and convincing way the word of God.

So I understood that radical change, which I as a bishop am supposed to make in my mind and in my pastoral activity, through conversations with Cardinal Bergoglio, because it was a big question for me: *What does it mean to be a Catholic bishop in Argentina?* And he explained it to me. For the first time, from him, I heard the word "pastoral conversion," meaning that you have to be a good shepherd, have a heart of a good pastor and not a prince of the Church, a pharaoh who is sitting on the golden chair. And I'm really grateful to him for my personal pastoral conversion, that the duty of a pastor is to heal the wounds. That means pastoral care; not to impose the rules but to heal the wounds, by the grace of the Holy Spirit. He told me: "In your hands, there is no possibility to impose things, but the Lord gave you the grace of the Holy Spirit to share." Well, it makes a real difference to propose different priorities, even to understand better who you are as a bishop and who you are as the one who is announcing the Good News to the world.

When he became pope, I understood this new image from that pastoral conversion. He said, "We're supposed to be a Church that goes out." The Church is a battlefield hospital which heals the wounds. A Church which with mercy is revealing an authentic message of the Gospel of our Lord Jesus Christ. A Church which by her nature is a neighbor to the modern human being. Who is my neighbor? The one who is showing mercy. So, love and mercy and care make us neighbors, not a physical coexistence with someone.

Regarding the people who were living in the bishop's residence and around the cathedral, that kind of closeness and pastoral care was part of our policy to help them be integrated into society and not always be maintained by the Church, but to give them a possibility to understand who they are and what they're supposed to do in that society outside of the Church walls. So that policy to go out even from those buildings was a part of the policy of the Church that goes out, like in the family: Father and mother rear children, but there comes a moment when those children have to leave the family. Not because father and mother do not want to take care of them, but because they have to be mature, they have to experience the world outside that very protective space of the parents. If not, they will forever be babies without the possibility to grow.

So that was a policy approaching those people who were for so many years staying there without any kind of life project for their families. It was not a simple intention to kick them out but to help them construct their own life project in Argentina.

7

Prayerful Decisions

John Burger: Cardinal Husar stepped down in 2011 due to health reasons. You and your fellow bishops from around the world made your way to Ukraine to elect a new major archbishop. What were you thinking and feeling as you went into this special meeting of the Synod of Bishops?

His Beatitude Sviatoslav: The general feeling among the bishops when Cardinal Husar stepped down was this: We were really concerned. There was some sort of fear, because looking around, I personally did not find anybody at the level of Cardinal Husar to be able to substitute for him in such a profound and significant level.

What was it about him that was in a way irreplaceable?

First of all, he was a patriarch, in the fullest sense of that word. He was an important moral authority for Ukrainian society. This was at the time of President Yanukovych, when there was renewed Russian pressure on independent Ukraine. And having Lubomyr as head of the Church, we were sure that the destiny of our people was in good hands, because of his authority and his profound wisdom, because of the great esteem in which everyone held him, both in Ukraine and abroad.

Suddenly, the "new Moses" of the Ukrainian nation disappeared, from our point of view. Of course, nobody knew at that time who would be able to substitute for him, according to those expectations that were inside of the synod, inside of our Church, and from outside the Church. At that time, I was the youngest among all the Ukrainian bishops, with no experience and no position. I was not even an ordinary bishop; I was the apostolic administrator of our eparchy in Argentina. We had metropolitans; we had some prominent personalities who were already known as moral authorities. I went to that electoral synod planning to go back home to Buenos Aires. My mission in Argentina had only started. I created much expectation from Ukrainians in Argentina, starting to reorganize our communities, providing pastoral care for abandoned parishes, providing pastoral care for vocations, and so on. So many people in Argentina were trusting me personally, and because of that personal relationship and trust, they had new hope, new expectations for that reorganization and renewal of our eparchy.

For me, it was not only a surprise but even a big disappointment that someone like me would draw the attention of my brother bishops for being able to substitute for such a patriarch as Lubomyr Husar was.

Why disappointment?

Because I felt that I had no experience, no capability good enough to lead such a global Church as the Ukrainian Greek Catholic Church; because of my age, and because I was not even able to understand which steps I was supposed to take first.

But I was led by the same feeling when I was elected a bishop and sent to Argentina: *If I will put as a primary goal my personal happiness and comfort, I would never accept.* But I felt that I would not seek my personal comfort. I would not seek some sort of security in my own imagination or my own ideas. If it is the will of God, not my desire, not because I want it, but because it was clear that the decision of the bishops is a sign of the manifestation of the will of God, I would accept.

Based on the discussions leading up to the vote and perhaps what other bishops have told you since then, can you tell me why you think you were chosen?

Sincerely, I don't know, even now. Because I think in the years since then — maybe every day — people ask themselves, "Why him? Is he special?" Definitely not!

I think it was a large amount of trust expressed on my behalf. But at the same moment, I told the bishops: "OK, I accept, but I will ask you to support me. Please don't leave me alone. Don't treat me like that goat of expiation in the Old Testament, because I'll be able to lead the Church only with you. We are a synodal Church, so, according to the principle of synodality, episcopal collegiality, please be with me."

And I have to say, the bishops responded. So, I am very grateful to my fellow bishops, especially in those very first moments, [that] they did not abandon me.

But also, it was encouraging that for the first time in history, my predecessor was with me. So His Beatitude Lubomyr did not abandon me. He was always very kind and open, but also, I would say, very sensitive in the way he assisted me, not giving the impression that he is still in charge. And it was a blessing to live with him almost four years in the same house, and we shared meals, prayer, conversations, even though he was retired as head of the Church, he was very active as a citizen of Ukraine, as a moral authority, as an important spiritual and intellectual personality.

In those circumstances, I was trying to support him, to make him more available to everybody who wanted to come and talk to him and meet him. It was a very open and transparent situation, with no competition, no jealousy, because I found that he was my spiritual father, as we met for the first time in the seminary, when he was our spiritual director. So I continued to have the same kind of relationship toward him. I was so blessed that he was with me, and I really felt deeply saddened when he passed away in May of 2017. Without his prayer, without his presence, it would have been very difficult for me to undertake especially those first moments of leadership in our Church.

Was the vote for you unanimous?

I cannot answer. Sorry. But I can say that the support of the bishops was really, really impressive.

What was the advice Cardinal Husar gave you when you were elected to succeed him?

His way to assist me was very special, I have to say. He would not give any advice. He let me ask him any kind of questions or for any kind of advice. And very often I would go to consult him in order to understand the origins of some phenomena we have in our Church.

Give me an example.

Well, perhaps we have some conflict. In order to understand, to make the right decision, I was asking him to help me understand how it started, what causes generated such a situation. And he was very kind to explain even the smallest details, even though he was blind. But his mind was so clear. He had all the information in his head. Otherwise, I would need to sit maybe days or even weeks reading documents and still not be sure if I understood those sources in the right way. But Lubomyr himself was the one who wrote many of those documents, and he was the one who gave me the right exegesis of that situation.

Did you find the office overwhelming at first? How did you cope?

Yes. First of all, I tried to keep my inner spiritual life, a life of prayer, and ask advice, even of my spiritual directors, who were in Rome, and their advice was to maintain the inner space of your freedom. That means you have to listen carefully to those who are around you, to those who are willing to assist you. But the responsibility is yours. You have to listen to everyone, especially those who would criticize you, because those who have the courage to criticize you are the people to whom you have to pay attention. Stay away from people who are willing to bring only good news and only agree with you, or always applaud you.

But, if someone is trying to impose on you some sort of policy or vision or decision, be careful, because their responsibility will be yours, not that person who is trying to push you toward such a decision.

I always tried to maintain that space of freedom, a space of reflection, and all those decisions which I made in those years were mine. And people realized very quickly that I am not just an external image. I am the authentic head of the Church, with the power to decide, and that was very important, especially in the beginning.

But it was also very important not only to have that space of freedom to make a decision, but also to take my time to think. It was also the policy of Lubomyr Husar. He used to say, "Well, we have to sleep on that." He was listening, but making decisions only the next day, because very often, emotions will go away overnight — your evening prayers, Divine Liturgy — and some clear ideas can come forward. And really, right now, very often, we live in the culture of not-well-matured decisions, and I learned especially from my predecessor that we have to give our decision a chance to mature. Like a piece of fruit: If it's ripe, it's ready to be eaten; if not, it can provoke some problems for the stomach.

You are the head of a synodal Church, that is, one governed by a synod of bishops. But what decisions are you able to make on your own, aside from that synod?

There are decisions for which I have to consult the whole synod, and it's supposed to be a decision of the synod. But very often, the head of the Church, according to Church law, has the competence to stop that decision — not to proclaim the decision of the synod — and it will not become law.

Can you give me an example, because a lot of people hear about synodality because Pope Francis talks about it so much.

Our concept of synodality is different from synodality in the Roman Catholic Church. For us, the synod is composed only of the bishops, and the Synod of Bishops has different competences. First of all, [it is] the highest tribunal of the Church — the high court. Then, the synod elects new bishops, and it is the highest Church body to legislate. Through the decision of this synod, we are developing our particular canon law. By myself, I cannot create some new laws of the Church that will be obligatory for the whole Church. Only the synod can. But if I don't proclaim that law, promulgate it with my decree, that decision would not be binding law.

Also, the synod makes some important decisions concerning the pastoral activity of the Church's liturgical life, creating new structures of the Church, because we have different branches of Church authority — legislative, judicial, and executive.

So basically, the synod is a legislative body, but also there is a Patriarchal Tribunal, and also the head of the Church is responsible for the executive branch. So it is my responsibility to create special structures in order to fulfill the decision of the synod, but also those decisions will become law for the executive branch only by my proclamation. So that is a very specific service of the head of the Church.

But also, the synod is always the gathering of the bishops with the head of the Church, so there are some things that the head of the Church cannot decide without the synod, for example, create new laws, elect new bishops, create new structures.

When you say new structures, does that include creating new eparchies?

New eparchies, new tribunals, and so on.

But also, bishops without the head of the Church are not a synod. Only when those two competences come together do we have the full body of the Church, capable of acting canonically, efficiently, with the whole authority given to the Church by Christ.

But also, the head of the Church, in my case, has three levels of responsibility, because the Ukrainian Catholic Church is at the same time a global Church as well as a local Church. Even the phrase "local Church" doesn't express well that sense that we understand from the term *sui iuris* — self-governing Church — because that terminology comes from the Roman Catholic point of view: local Church means only your diocese. But for us, the local Church is not only the eparchy. The head of the Church has three levels of duty: He is a bishop of an eparchy, but also, he is the leader of the episcopate in Ukraine, and also, he is the leader of the worldwide Church.

So even on the local level, the level of our country, the responsibility of the head of the Church goes beyond the boundaries of his own eparchy. But also, his responsibility goes beyond the borders of Ukraine, even if the way to exercise his jurisdiction inside Ukraine and outside of the country is different, according to the prescriptions of canon law.

For example, you cannot on your own appoint bishops to places like Chicago or Sydney.

For example, I have the personal jurisdiction to celebrate a marriage throughout the whole world. But it's my personal responsibility; I cannot delegate it to someone else.

So the pastoral care for the faithful of our Church who are outside the structures of our Church is a personal responsibility of the head of the Church. There are some countries where we do not even have a parish, but we have our faithful. So to whom are they supposed to ask for adequate pastoral care? To me. I have to think of how to provide them with adequate pastoral care. Of course, I'll visit them; of course, I'll send my representatives to study the situation. But afterwards, if I want to send a priest to that place, I have to enter into contact with the local Roman Catholic bishop, because I cannot directly delegate my jurisdiction to that priest in that country, but only through the pastoral ministry of the local bishop, even if that bishop is not a member of our Church.

And of course, when we have to create a structure in such a country, we have to consult the Holy See, because that presence would not be an isolated Church structure only for our Church, but that bishop, that priest, will be a member of the Catholic communion with other Churches that belong to the Catholic communion in that country.

I can offer many examples of how it started in our history, but it was always like that. The head of the Church was trying to offer adequate pastoral care to his faithful in that country, so he was visiting them. Then he was trying to establish contact with the local Roman Catholic bishop, asking him to accept a priest, whom I would send there, and that parish would be like the first germ of the development of our presence in that particular country.

The Ukrainian Greek Catholic Church has spread to so many places around the globe. How many frequent flier miles did you accumulate last year?

When I was elected, I promised that I would visit everybody, but I have to say that even though I've been traveling now [in 2019] for almost eight years, I have not yet visited everybody. Basically, I've visited all our eparchies — in Australia, Argentina, Brazil, the United States, Canada, Western Europe, Central Europe, Kazakhstan, and other countries.

But also, in order to help me assist those who are outside of our Church structures, I have a special department for the pastoral care of migrants. My auxiliary bishop of Kyiv is in charge of that, and he is helping me to visit.

I don't remember exactly how many miles I accumulated last year, but at least two trips I get for free.

On average, how often do you go to the airport?

Maybe twice a month. But I'm trying to follow the instructions of Pope Francis, who asks bishops not to be bishops of airports.

Still, it's not so easy for me, because I'm head of a global Church, and those visits are part of my duty. It is how I have to build the inner communion between different parts of the Ukrainian Greek Catholic Church. We communicate each day with various tools, but in many cases, you have to have personal meetings, personal visits, personal conversations. You cannot substitute that. People want to — and have the right to — meet personally with the head of the Church. I'm trying to respond to those needs and be a good pastor for them.

What do you mean by "inner communion," and why is this an issue?

The inner communion of a Church is a personal relationship with the head of the Church, who is a visible sign and a servant of that communion. That kind of communion I call "inner" because it is cherished within the community of our Church. However, this communion can be fully understood only in relation with the universal communion of the Catholic Church experienced by a full and visible communion with the successor of Saint Peter the apostle. The head of the [local, particular] Church is also a servant, promoter, and preacher of that communion with the successor of Saint Peter.

Do you still feel a little overwhelmed or maybe even scared by the realization that, "Oh my goodness, I'm responsible for this whole global Church"?

I have to say that each day, I'm rediscovering how big our Church is, and I'm really scared. But fear, according to the Book of Wisdom, is the beginning of wisdom. That feeling that you are standing in front of something which overcomes you, something which is really out of your direct control. But that Church is the Body of Christ. So what gives me courage very often is that very fundamental ecclesiological vision that not I, but Christ is the head of the Church. And I always say: "OK, my Savior, this is *your* Church, this is *your* Bride, and *you* are the Bridegroom. I'm in your service; I'm your visible representative for my Church, but I'm only human. Only you are everywhere present, and I am conscious of my human limitations. So please help me, and I'll try to do my best."

So I think that humility is very important — to recognize your limits. And it gives you also a possibility to delegate your duties, to find the people to whom you can entrust different responsibilities.

When in the Divine Liturgy you pray for a peaceful death and a "good defense at the awesome tribunal of Christ," are you ever struck by the feeling that, "My God, I have all this responsibility, and I'll have to answer for all this one day"?

Of course, you're right, because each day you discover not only the dimension of your Church but your own responsibilities as well. And well, it is scary.

But I'm a moral theologian, and moral theology says that if you freely and consciously neglect your duties, you can be punished. It's your fault. But if you are rediscovering your duties and you are aware of them and you are aware that you are not able to fulfill them, you have to find a solution, and it provokes you to develop a policy, to build structures, to find new people to trust that part of your personal responsibility, because I think it is a very important part of the art of administration not to accumulate everything in your hands. If you don't trust anybody and you try to do everything yourself, you will be exhausted in one day, and you will be a very inefficient administrator.

And we find examples in the word of God. When Moses was trying to intervene with each case that people presented to him, his father-in-law suggested that he choose good people who can judge the cases, and if there is some extraordinary case, they will bring it to you. Because otherwise, you will not be able to fulfill your administration and lead your people to the final destination. I find that example providential, and I think every good leader, not only of the Church, has to be humble enough to delegate his authority to others in order to have the possibility to fulfill his mission.

With all this responsibility, how do you care for your own spiritual health?

There are three rules — and I try to keep them in whatever situation I'm in. I was taught these rules in the underground Church.

First rule: You have to celebrate the Divine Liturgy daily, except on those days that are aliturgical[1] according to our tradition.

Second: Pray a Divine Office each day, because the Divine Office is not your private prayer, but praying the Divine Office, you are praying with the Church, for the Church, but also inside the Church, even if you are alone.

Third: daily meditation on the divine word.

So, Eucharist, Divine Office as a prayer of the Church community, and meditating on the divine word — reading Holy Scripture and meditation.

Those three rules were fundamental in the most dramatic situations in the history of our Church. Even in prison, our priests celebrated the Divine Liturgy daily. I remember a visit from a priest to our seminary in Rudno, when I was a seminarian. His name was Fr. Ivan Margitich. He was ordained in the concentration camp by Patriarch Josyf Slipyj, and immediately on the next day, Patriarch Josyf approached him asking, "Did you celebrate Divine Liturgy today?" He responded, "No." And the reaction of the Patriarch was, "Oh God, why did I ordain you?"

The priest asked how priests could celebrate Divine Liturgy in prison, with no chalice or other liturgical vessels. And Patriarch Josyf took off his glasses and said [pointing to each lens], "That is a chalice. That is a paten. One drop of wine and one small piece of bread. And your hand is the altar."

So I understood that our Church survived as a Church because of the Eucharist. And the Eucharist is a summit but also the source of the Church's life.

Very often, when I'm traveling, coming back home at the end of the day, I always try to find time to celebrate Divine Liturgy.

Second, the Divine Office. Really, I have to say that very often, priests today neglect that privilege and treat it as a burden. But the Divine Office makes you feel like you are part of a big community, and very often you feel that you need some help. But praying with the Church, you are receiving that help. If you feel lonely, praying the Divine Office will make you feel like you are part of a big global community.

---

1. When the Church does not normally have Mass.

But also, the first and most important duty of the priest or bishop is not to administrate your community but to pray for your people. And if you pray the Divine Office, you are fulfilling your most important duty — you are praying for your flock.

And third, without daily meditation on the divine word, you will not receive enough spiritual nourishment. And you will not have a word in your heart and mouth to proclaim. As a bishop, you are supposed to be in his service, dedicated especially to the proclamation of the word of God. How can you give without being able to receive? You can give not your own word but the word of God only if you receive that divine word. You chew on that word, you digest it, you appropriate it. You are in your own personal dialogue with God through his word. Only in this way will you have his word that he wants you to transmit to the people.

Can you describe how that works — the daily meditation on the word of God? How can people go deeper than the words on the page?

I use different tools. There are some aids for daily meditation — daily text of the Holy Scripture and some texts of the Holy Fathers. Even on your iPhone you have access to the Bible. It's not so difficult today.

That kind of meditation is like *lectio divina*. You take some text — it doesn't matter which one — and you listen carefully to what the text is saying to you, because it's a Person of the Divine Trinity that is speaking to you through that text.

Then you ask, "How can I respond to that with my life? How can I transmit or witness to that word of God to others?"

And it's crucial to have daily contact with the word of God — reading, meditating, and praying with the divine word.

How long do you do this for?

It has to be a part of your daily life. In our normal life here at the Patriarchal Residence, we pray Matins and Divine Liturgy in the morning and Vespers in the late afternoon. On an average day, I try to find at least a half hour to read the word of God and to meditate on it. Normally, I have the possibility to do that before work in the office begins, because when people come to work, forget it. It's very distracting, almost impossible to do it.

Do you feel like you have to read a certain amount, or, let's say you read one line and it says so much to you in that one line that you could sit and think about that for a while?

Normally, you have to read a section, because you cannot pick up a phrase out of context.

Let me ask you if you have a regular confessor or spiritual director.

I have to make a distinction between confessor and spiritual director. I try to confess frequently. It depends: Sometimes you've committed more sins, sometimes you're more stable in your behavior. But I try to approach confession at least once a week. I try to confess frequently in order to be in the grace of God, in order to celebrate the sacraments with dignity and so on. This is my personal way to live the spiritual life.

To have frequent access to your spiritual advisor or director is not so easy. I have my spiritual advisor in Rome, so I try to find time to talk to him.

Sometimes, confession can be combined with spiritual direction, sometimes not. But they are two different realities.

Can you tell us anything about your spiritual director?

Well, I prefer not to name him, but he knows me very well from over the years. He is a father, not a simple friend. He's very frank and direct, but authentic.

And I have to say, it's not easy to find a spiritual director. But if you find him, consider him a gift of God — a holy man given to you by God. And you have to follow his directions. If you think you know better than your spiritual director, this is the wrong way to consider yourself.

How often do you go on retreat?

At least once a year, we have a retreat. Normally, we organize a retreat for all Catholic bishops in Ukraine — both Roman Catholics and Byzantine Catholics. Normally, we'll stay together for a week, inviting a preacher. One year, it's my duty to prepare that retreat and find somebody to lead it; another year it's the duty of the president of the Roman Catholic bishops' conference. And when it's my duty, we host the bishops in our retreat center. When it's the Roman Catholic bishops' conference, they host us in their center. It's usually in the second part of November, when we are approaching Advent.

So it's not the case that you go on retreat by yourself?

Sometimes I do, because sometimes you have a special feeling that you need such a retreat, because you're not able to continue normally. You need to recover your spiritual life or your equilibrium.

For you, what is an ideal retreat, whether it's for a priest or a lay person?

To be disconnected from your daily life and to be totally focused on the person of God, to dedicate that time exclusively for him, because very often we simply are not able to listen to him, and we need a time to be disconnected from the world in order to open our ears and listen to the Savior.

Have you ever gone on retreat in an Orthodox monastery? Have you ever gone to Mount Athos in Greece, for example?

Among the Orthodox, they don't have such retreats. They would have pilgrimages. They would offer a possibility to have a spiritual conversation. They would offer the possibility just to stay with them a few days — a week, if you wish. But not a regular retreat as we understand it according to the tradition of the Catholic Church. So nobody would preach to you each day, preparing conferences and so on.

I used to visit some Orthodox monasteries, but it's not easy to find somebody willing to talk to you, because they would consider you a stranger, a heretic, someone to tolerate your presence but not to be engaged in your spiritual health.

Why a heretic?

For them Catholics are heretics. They consider Catholics as non-Orthodox, which means heretic.

I've never been on Mount Athos. I tried several times when I was in Greece, but because I'm from Ukraine, and because in my passport I had a photo of myself in a Roman collar, I never got a visa to visit Mount Athos.

But even though the Orthodox don't "give" retreats in the sense that we understand in the Western Church, an Orthodox monastery is a good place to disconnect, wouldn't you say?

Definitely. But today, you have to exercise some discipline to be disconnected, because even in the Orthodox monasteries, there is cellular coverage, and with your iPhone you can be connected to the internet. And someone will find you, sooner or later.

And when you know there's Wi-Fi available, you can be constantly thinking about connecting to the internet. You might be able to disconnect for a while, but then you're like, "Oh, let me just check this one thing," and that leads to something else, and before you know it, you're fully engaged with the digital world.

Yes, but also, there's some sort of dependence on that connection. We are addicted to that connection, to that information. And very often, there is some sort of false security: If you are informed, *everybody's OK; everything's OK.* If you don't know something, well, *something must be happening.* If you're not looking at the internet, not receiving news, something tragic can happen.

But it's just an illusion.

Are you a big internet user? Are you active on social media?

I'm not present in social media. I receive information through email, by reading official websites, and by meetings and regularly reading correspondence. I found that to be constantly present in social media is very uncomfortable, because it takes a lot of time without any kind of selectivity about the information you're receiving.

Nevertheless, I try to be available and open and communicate with the world on a regular basis, but you need discernment. I offered my secretariat the responsibility to select the information that comes in, according to certain principles. But I try to read all the letters that are addressed to me.

What about reading — what kinds of books do you read?

I really enjoy reading historical books. History is my passion, because I'm convinced that *Historia magistra vitae est*: History is a teacher of life. And very often, we can understand what is going on and why it is happening if we know the history — the *authentic* history.

Last year [2018], there were many books published with documents which earlier were not accessible, for example about the destruction of our Church, documents of some specific period or concerning specific personalities, some historical studies on the most important events. In 2017, we marked the one hundredth anniversary of the so-called Bolshevik Revolution, and I really enjoyed reading many studies of that period, and I realized how manipulated we were when we studied that in the Soviet schools. Also, concerning the Holodomor, even today, each year there is new information coming out.

I also enjoy reading theological books. I really miss teaching. Any time I go to Rome, I try to visit the students and ask them about new works. Regularly, I try to see new patristic studies, because patristics is part of our identity as a [Byzantine] Church, but also studies on moral theology, because it's my academic interest.

8

Building Community

John Burger: You are faced with many decisions in your position. Tell me about the process you experience in making tough decisions. How does prayer come into play?

His Beatitude Sviatoslav: First of all, I try to make a space where that decision can mature. And discussion with the experts, people who are very competent on a particular issue, is very important.

But also, making a space means to present that issue to God as well. That's why, according to the methodology of Cardinal Husar, we have to come through the night with that discernment, that decision, because coming through the night, you will bring that decision to God in the time of Vespers, in the time of Matins, Divine Liturgy, and meditation on the word of God. And that process is an integral part of the process of discernment, because in order to make a decision, you have to discern. Consulting people, we reflect, but then you have to discern, and according to Byzantine spirituality, discernment is not only an intellectual process, it also goes through a discernment of spirits. So, there is always some spiritual foundation to many phenomena in life.

What is prayer for you? Describe a typical time of prayer.

Prayer is a conversation with God. It's a dialogue. It's an interpersonal relationship. There's common prayer — Divine Office, Divine Liturgy — but also personal prayer. Not private, but personal. And I would articulate my personal prayer in five steps.

I start with a prayer of thanksgiving, which always has two parts: thanksgiving for creation and thanksgiving for salvation. It is very important to realize that we are creatures, and we are standing before our Creator, the source of our life and being. He's not a simple friend to speak to. No — he's the source of my existence. And secondly, he's my Savior. So that thanksgiving goes to the Father, because of the gift of his Son, made accessible to me through the gift of the Holy Spirit.

This is the first step.

Second is the prayer of repentance. Standing in front of the Holy One, you have to be conscious that you are a sinner. According to the Eastern spirituality, our spiritual progress is the development of the likeness of God in me. We are created in the image of God, but all those dissimilarities reveal my sinfulness. Repentance is the way to approach God. Our movement toward him is repentance, not a simple juridical punishment for your failures, but your approach to him and your understanding of the distance you have to overcome reveals your sinfulness.

The third step is prayer for the others, prayer for my neighbors, prayer for the needs of the Church, prayer for the needs of particular people who ask for prayer, prayer for those entrusted to your pastoral care and for whom you are responsible.

Only then comes a fourth step: prayer for my own intentions, my own needs. First neighbor, then self. Of course, we bring to God our needs. We need his help.

The fifth step, like a conclusion of that prayer, is a prayer of glorification of God. That is the summit of our prayer. We glorify him not because we receive from him but because his glory is eternal. And I always ask him, "Lord, you made me a participant of your glorification here on earth, in front of your earthly altar. Make me part of the Divine Liturgy in heaven. Make me worthy to glorify you with your saints and angels in heaven."

All those intentions and all those questions of discernment I try to pass through those five stages, because the final goal of the mission of the Church, of my decision, my life, is *ad majorem Dei gloriam* ["to the greater glory of God"] — the only motivation, the sole reason for my mission, my activity, my life.

From the spiritual, let's turn to the physical. Is exercise important for you? Is it even possible to exercise, given your schedule and responsibilities?

Yes, I try each day, as a part of my schedule, to reserve at least an hour to do physical exercises. When I'm home, that's part of my normal life. I'm a jogger. But if you're traveling, it's not so easy. But nevertheless, I try to find a moment to walk, to move, not to sit.

You're not married, and you don't have children. How do you try to stay in touch with the normal, everyday life of lay people, most of whom have families, with all the concerns and sufferings that go along with that?

To meet them. To share with them. To visit them. I cherish very much many friendships that I have. I do have good friends — not too many, because I think that if you have hundreds of friends, it means that you have nobody as your real friend. But there are some people with whom I share my life, my concerns, my joys, but also, I try to participate in their joys and their life, and listen to them. For me, it's important to have lots of different points of view to consider the situation of our Church in Ukraine and so on.

Very often, I feel there's not enough time to stay together, but each moment I can find, I try to dedicate to them.

But also, I'm still really blessed to have a family — my mother and father.[1] They are very important for me, even if I don't have the possibility to

---

[1]. His Beatitude's mother passed away in April 2021.

visit them frequently. But each day, we communicate through Skype, so we can share, we can talk, we can see each other, we can reflect together, make decisions together, and so on.

But I think those human relationships are vital for us. If not, there's a big risk that we become like machines. And it's also very important to share your emotions. OK, you are sad, but you need to express your sadness. You are joyful, but you need to express, share your joy with somebody.

You talk about friends. We all know that the term friend is used very loosely, and that there are different kinds of friends in life. A really good friend, however, is a pearl of great price. How does the world today regard the concept of friends in general? Have we lost the ability to cultivate really good friendships in our lives, and in what ways does that lead to suffering? What advice would you give people about friendship, about finding it, discerning it, maintaining it?

Friendship is something without which we cannot be ourselves. We cannot be a friend with everybody. We can be friendly. But I think that real friends — there are few around you. Why? Because a friend is somebody who is part of my personal story, somebody to whom I would relate my personal thoughts and even intentions, someone who cares about me, and I care about him.

So a friend is a very important person. There is a whole philosophy about friendship and what it means. According to the Neoplatonic tradition, we are supposed to be a friend of God. Why? Because growing our similarity with and likeness to God, we would become more and more like him, and friends are supposed to be similar. Similarity is a foundation of friendship. We are on the same wavelength. This is why when a friend betrays me, it is a very painful experience, because it is like someone cutting out a part of myself. It's why Christ would say, "There is no greater love than someone who lays down his life for his friend." That's why I do have friends, friends with whom I can be myself, be confident. We can talk about all issues, and I can feel safe, confident that they will not reveal my secrets to the whole world. They would not betray me.

I think we have to have friends, because a person by his inner construction is supposed to always be an outgoing person. We need someone to go out toward. Otherwise, we can become very self-centered. It's why we have to cherish friendship very much, to cultivate friendship.

Also, you are right to say that today, the word *friend* is very instrumentalized. The whole system of friends in our "networked society" is changing, because a friend is someone with whom I am in contact. We can be in contact with the whole world, but human relations can be very poor.

So, connection, to be a member of a group, to be a "follower" of somebody doesn't mean to be a friend at all. It is why a human relationship makes me a friend with a person I care about — his feelings, his story, his joy and sorrow are part of my own feelings, pains, and joys. That kind of interpersonal communion, I think, is a cornerstone of authentic friendship.

We talked about digital technology and social media. I wonder if this is part of the reason we're seeing so much more depression and even suicide, even among young people, because they think they have a lot of friends on Facebook, for example. But is that taking the place of real friendship?

I think that nothing, even spiritual relationships, can substitute for an authentic interpersonal relationship. I think that this huge explosion of modern technology and new ways to communicate with people leads us to underestimate friendship as such, and I hope that one day we can rediscover friendship and learn what it means to be a friend. Because to be a friend means not only to receive something from my friends, but also to be able to give something — my time, my attention — to understand that his good is my concern.

And cell phones have invaded childhood — from an early age. Kids are growing up staring at screens rather than playing with friends. You sometimes see a parent try to take a phone away from a small child, and he's yelling and kicking. You can walk into a room of kids, and no one looks up from his phone to greet you. Often, it seems, they're not even talking to one another. It's very different from the way we grew up.

Me, too. We would be playing outside. To stay home alone was a punishment: "Today, you will not go to play because you did that." But today, to be forced to play with somebody else could be a punishment.

In the [Vatican] Synod on Young People, the Faith, and Vocational Discernment [in Rome, October 2018], we discussed how that new technological revolution creates difficulties in the capability to relate to others, but also, we very often relate our own capacities with the capacities of the computer.

An example I heard at the synod: A two-year-old child knew very well how to use an iPad, to go from one page to another [scrolling down the screen with the finger], looking for different pictures. But the iPad was taken away and the child received a simple printed book, and he was trying to change a page by using the same action he was using on the iPad. He was performing that action, but the page was not changing. The kid started to look at his finger [quizzically]. So the first thought is, "There's something wrong with me. My body is not working." It's why even today, in bioethics, there is a whole issue of the cybernetization of the human body, because we consider our body as a machine. And that affects many other things.

I have a friend who is a dentist. Several years ago, he was telling me that for the dentist to extract your tooth would make him feel like a loser. *He lost his battle with some illness that affected his tooth.* But today, that's not the case anymore. Today, the dentist would look into the mouth of a person and say, "Oh, you have too many teeth. I have to extract some, and I would advise you to get an implant." The same with the knees. Who would spend years and years helping you heal your knees? They would rather replace them with artificial ones.

So we are starting to consider our body as a machine, and we're trying to substitute the bad parts of the organism for a cyber system that will help your body function better. But my body is not a machine; my body is part of my person. A human being is an incarnated soul or a spiritualized body. My body has to be respected, because it's a temple of the Holy Spirit. My body was created for eternal life, and we as Christians believe in the resurrection of the body. So that ideology of the cyber transformation of the human body has to be transformed by Christian anthropology. It's a big challenge.

But you wouldn't say that an artificial knee is a bad thing. They've helped a lot of people with restored mobility.

No, absolutely. It can help people. But we need to understand that our body is not a simple *thing*. It's a part of my person. It's me. So if the medical assistance helps me to be healthy, to live better and longer, that is medical care, but care of my person.

That's why that integral anthropology, including the well-being of my body, is so important.

What are your personal fears?

I have no fears concerning myself, but very often I can feel some fears for others, especially for my country, for my people, because war is the biggest concern.[2] There are so many wounds, so much pain inside the Church. Will it get worse? Will we be able to give an adequate response to that new challenge?

What things do you not like about yourself — areas where you feel you need improvement?

I need improvement to be more patient with people. Very often, I feel I am too self-demanding, and I can be very demanding toward others, so I have to be more merciful, to understand that, *OK, maybe people simply can't follow you. There's somebody who's weaker than you are. You have to understand that somebody is not doing things right, not because he doesn't want to but for some reason just can't.*

So, very often, I would confess my sins of failing in love for my neighbors, but also very often, you have to comment on the behavior of others. The judgment of others also can be a part of my failures, because we judge according to external observation, but very often, we have no time or even interest to go inside of the personal situation of the person.

It's also not very easy to combine the institutional policy with the

---

2. At the time of this interview, in May 2019, Ukraine had been fighting a Russia-backed separatist movement in the Eastern oblasts of Donetsk and Luhansk — the Donbas. Before the 2022 full-scale invasion of Ukraine, the Donbas conflict had already claimed some fourteen thousand lives.

personal situation of those people who are working in that institution. There are some interests of the community, but also some private interests of each member of that community. How to combine them — private, personal, and communitarian? Because very often, we are driven by our egoism. In modern culture, there is a big temptation of fragmentation of the community, fragmentation of the human experience as well, because individualistic society goes against the principle of community life. And Church is community.

So how to be one who is able, and whose duty it is, to build community? It's a big challenge today.

And I feel that very often, even inside our communities, people feel lonely. Loneliness today is one of the biggest problems, not only in the Church but in society as well. Very often, we communicate very intensively. We are in touch with the whole world. But human relationships are very poor, and people feel lonely. Very often, the addiction to that [social media–based] communication can be the fruit of that loneliness. Very often, we live our life paying attention to the world outside of ourselves, and very often, we're afraid to look inside and encounter the authentic self. And I think that each pastor, each spiritual leader, first of all has to be the person who has that charism, that art, to help people be themselves, be authentic.

How can pastors help people be themselves?

This is related to the statement of Cardinal Bergoglio saying an authentic pastor has to heal the wounds. Each of us is a fruit of his own history, and we are asking for medical care when we feel physical pain; we need to be cured. But also, I think we have to have a good spiritual guide in order to heal our spiritual wounds.

Relating to the situation in Ukraine, we don't realize how deeply wounded our nation is by the war. But also, we understand that physical wounds, such as bullet wounds, are materialized evil and would hurt me, but there are many different kinds of bullets of evil that hit me every day. My evil action wounds me before I can hurt someone else. Any evil thoughts hurt me.

So evil is not neutral. Evil destroys. But first of all, it destroys someone who is absorbing that evil and making it part of his own style of life. Today, we don't even understand how deeply wounded we are as human beings because of very subtle new forms of evil which affect us. And very often, we are not able to discern, and spiritual direction helps us discern between good and evil. It's basic discernment that makes us a mature people. A person who cannot discern between good and evil is an eternal baby, someone who has no basic possibilities to grow. The next discernment is between authentic and fake good. To have a capacity to discern between what is authentic and what is fake is the next step of maturity. If I'm willing to do good, is that good authentic or some sort of manipulation of the notion of the good?

Maybe a self-serving notion of goodness — something that appears to be altruistic but is really meant to advance one's own interest?

Absolutely. That is the way to happiness, if we are able to detect authentic good, and if we are able to incarnate that good in our own life, our thoughts, intentions, actions.

That is why we need spiritual guidance, because on our own, we will not be able to grow in those steps of discernment. We can learn how to discern well only in the context of a dialogue with someone. Ultimately, the dialogue is supposed to be our dialogue with God, because he is the one who created good. He is the Good, with a capital *G*. And to have a possibility to converse with him, to talk to him, to pray, we receive a capacity of discernment between good and evil, and authentic good, the best way to reach that good that we are looking for, and how that good with a small *g* is related to the plenitude, to the Good with a capital *G*. Every important action that makes us grow, we have to learn how to do it, because we are human beings with free will, with reason, called to be personally responsible for our actions, but we need to learn how to do that, and spiritual direction helps us to do that, to learn how. We have to have a good teacher to learn how to read and write; we need a good coach to learn how to play basketball well and not hurt ourselves. Maybe we need good psychological counseling in order to learn how to deal with our emotions, with our comprehension of the world around us and our relations with other people. But also, we need good spiritual guidance and pastoral care in order to do good and avoid evil.

When you talk about things like your struggle with impatience, it seems that God allows us to have certain undesirable traits so that we have something to work on; it helps us realize that we do need to work in certain areas of our lives on our way to sanctity. When we pray in the Lord's Prayer, "Give us this day our daily bread," could we not consider such struggles to be our daily bread — the areas in which we can exercise the virtues and build up the "muscles" of our soul?

Very often, when I go through that second step of my personal prayer, the prayer of forgiveness, I always try to figure out those weaknesses I have as a person. Often, I ask him, "Lord, show me my weaknesses. Can you help me comprehend my faults?" I was taught that each time God shows you your sin, helps you to comprehend your sinfulness, this also is a kind of mercy toward you, because the biggest problem, when someone thinks he is sinless — "I am perfect" — the problem always is that "others are bad and I am good." It's a big illusion, and the biggest manifestation of that illusion is pride. In order to help you be humble, God gives you the grace to see your weaknesses.

There's a nice image from Saint Augustine. He compared the human heart — the inner world — with chambers below the earth. Those chambers are hidden. You cannot see them, even if you go below the earth. In order to discover them and have a clear image, you need a light. You need a torch. You can see that chamber inasmuch as that torch illuminates it.

That torch is the grace of God, the word of God. You have to go inside of your inner chambers, lighting them with that divine light. Jesus said, "I am the light of the world." Each time you go inside with this light, you will find some darkness, some sinfulness. But the very fact that you did discover it is the grace of God. And I think it's very important to learn to not be afraid to discover this sin, because according to Eastern spirituality, if you discover your sin and you expose it to the grace of God, that evil loses its strength.

OK, maybe you committed a sin — a bad one. If you try to cover it up, that sin will grow. But if you try to reveal it, to expose it to the grace of God, it will disappear. It will lose its strength. Revealing the sin, we make it weak. Very often, we cannot simply overcome sin. We need salvation, and we need to be liberated by someone, but the condition for that liberation is to reveal your weakness.

And I have to testify that I proved that that is true. I lived many situations where, if I hid that from God, from my confessor, from my spiritual father, I would be a slave to that sin, that weakness, that addiction. But at the very moment, even when I made the decision to present the situation, I felt free.

It seems like that's a good answer to people who don't understand why they should confess their sins to a priest, rather than going "straight to God."

If you say, "I can present it straight to God," my question is, "Will you be able to do that by yourself?" Maybe you are simply hiding that sin, only covering it in your personal background. But you have to reveal it to somebody. It's why God sends his representatives, because you have to reveal to another person.

It was a special tradition among the Desert Fathers to reveal your thoughts to your spiritual father, not only your deeds, your sins committed by some actions, but even some thoughts, because very often, first of all we will fall to sinful thoughts, and if you reveal your thoughts to your spiritual father, he will help you overcome evil thoughts but also help you make a discernment; he will help you know yourself better and not to incarnate that thought in your action, because otherwise, the evil will go through your heart and will damage not only your mind and your imagination but also your heart, your body, your person.

9

Healing Sin and Wounds

John Burger: Is the Church doing what Jesus asked? Is she evangelizing as she ought?

His Beatitude Sviatoslav: It's a good question. I have to say that I don't know, because in order to answer, you have to know everything, to be aware of each part of the Church life in the whole world. And I think we will receive such a notion only in the last, terrible judgment, when Christ will come in his second and glorious coming.

But I think that we have to distinguish between Church as a community — a global community — and Church as a structure. And we can argue if the Church as a structure is efficient or not, efficient to achieve that mission given to her by Christ or not, according to today's circumstances. And I think we have to consider that question each day, especially when we as bishops gather in our synods, when we as consecrated persons are making some evaluation of our mission, our communities, when we are trying to understand if our parish is vibrant or not.

And that question, we have to ask ourselves as Christians, because I am a member of the Church, and I am responsible for my Church. If I evangelize, the Church evangelizes. If I am faithful to my vocation, I make the Church faithful to her vocation. If I deny Christ through my everyday decisions and actions, that means I'm failing in front of the mission of the whole Church as well.

Do you ever have the feeling that the Church is not teaching everything it ought to? For example, on Good Friday we commemorate the crucifix-ion. But do most people understand just why Jesus died on the cross? Are pastors making it clear? Do people even care? Do more and more people dismiss it as a legend?

I think the mission of the Church is not to explain everything, because very often, we simply cannot. The paschal mystery — the passion, death, and resurrection of Christ — we call a mystery, which is not something secret, hidden. But simply, anytime we try to understand why, we feel we cannot comprehend fully, because that mystery is so deep and wide that any explanation will be insufficient. It's why we call it the mystery of the Church. It's something that is so big, but we are in-vited to come in, to be a part, to participate, to partake in that mystery.

The original mission, or kerygma, of the Church was to announce, to make known that event, to make known to everybody that that happened, that really happened. And that happened for me, because of me. And I can say that, well, the Church is announcing that event until our times, and the Church as a community of believers experiences that that event not only happened in the past but is accessible to us today, so we can be witnesses of the passion, death, and resurrection of Christ, even today.

Even when Jesus was dying on the cross, many people didn't care. Perhaps we can assume that many people did not believe, or considered the news as foolish, irrelevant for them. The same is happening today. Christ is present among us — really, authentically present. We speak about a "Real Presence" of Christ in the holy Eucharist. But nevertheless, you have to believe in that. You are invited. Saint Augustine says, "I be-lieve in order to understand, and I try to understand in order to believe."

My comprehension of that event is growing through my faith. Pope John Paul II, in one of the Masses he celebrated for students, gave this example: We know that modern aircraft can reach very high altitudes and fly at the speed of sound or faster. But they have limits they cannot overcome. Humans can experience that limit to comprehend the mystery of salvation. But what is happening? God goes forth, meeting us, and he by the power of the Holy Spirit takes that aircraft or those human capabilities and makes it possible to overcome limits. That's why reason and faith are compatible. We have to search; we have to be curious. But we have to understand that without God's help, without the grace of the Holy Spirit, we cannot enjoy the whole mystery of his love for us.

But does the Church emphasize enough this connection between the crucifixion and the original sin of Adam, that it could only be God who could be capable of paying for that sin — and therefore, the Incarnation, God-become-man, Jesus Christ?

I'm convinced that any achievement of our catechesis or our pastoral care we cannot consider as sufficient. It was an observation of Pope Benedict XVI that, even with the development of communication, the development of possibilities to know the basic foundation of the Christian Faith, religious ignorance is growing each year in the world. So even Catholics — Christians in all denominations — are becoming more and more ignorant of the basic foundation of Christian identity.

What is happening? Don't we teach adequately or properly? People are becoming more and more insensitive to religious issues. Do we emphasize more those connections between the death and resurrection of Christ and original sin? But also my personal salvation in Christ? Of course. Will it be enough? Maybe not.

As we discussed, you knew Cardinal Bergoglio in Argentina. As you have watched him since his election to the papacy in March 2013, in what ways has he changed from the man you knew in Buenos Aires?

He smiles. I see him more joyful, more open today. In Argentina, he looked very concerned and very often severe. I remember his way of communicating. He was very clear, but very short in his homilies and speeches. I remember his homily when Argentina celebrated two hundred years of independence. It was in 2010, and he presided at that celebration as the president of the bishops' conference. In his homily, he delivered five sentences. Maybe six. But each sentence was like a bullet — very impressive, very deep.

Today, I see him more open, more eloquent even. He is more himself, maybe, transformed by the power of the Holy Spirit.

But he was always very devoted to the Divine Mercy. He was very severe with himself, very demanding of bishops and priests, but very merciful toward sinners. Even the word of Divine Mercy is in his coat of arms, and now he is like [*sic*] developing that devotion, making that devotion a central part of his ministry.

In what ways?

That mercy toward the weaknesses of the wounded human being in today's world. We might say, "Well, mercy is like relativism of the rules." But it's not true. He is really concerned about how to heal those who are wounded.

So, his approach, I can say, is a therapeutic one, very close to my way of considering reality. A doctor always will try to avoid the worst. He will always try to find an adequate medicine in order to heal — not to condemn the patient because he's sick, but to find appropriate medicine in order to restore his health.

Very often, the prudent doctor will administer various medicines with different strengths. Sometimes, you have to act radically; sometimes you have to be very tender; sometimes you have to use strong medicine, sometimes a light one. That kind of pastoral prudence is an integral part of Eastern spirituality. The spirituality of the Christian is by its definition a therapeutic one. So spiritual care is considered a spiritual healing. The sacraments are like medications. Divine grace is that healing power which the Church has. We are all sinners, but we are in the Church, which is like a field hospital, to use Pope Francis's expression.

Eastern spirituality uses two ways to treat a sinner. One is [the Greek word] *akribeia*, which means a very exact and even merciless application of some laws and norms, because the sinner really needs that. *Your situation is really bad, and we have to act decisively and radically. You have no choice. You will adopt such measures, or you will die.*

The other approach is *epikeia*, which means condescendence. It means a merciful application. So, the law of gradation: I can see you will not be able to bear those heavy things I am imposing on your shoulders, so I will give you a less heavy one. But you have to work and grow in order to be able to bear heavier and heavier burdens. You will receive that more solid food, according to your capability to digest it.

So, two approaches: *akribeia* — very exact application of the norms — and *epikeia* — condescension, mercifulness, the application of some light medicine in order to help you heal and help you become able to fulfill more difficult rules.

These two kinds of possibilities go together. They are in the hands of the spiritual father, who considers your personal situation. He is like a spiritual healer, a doctor, and he discerns what kind of medicine to administer to you.

Is this how Pope Francis is thinking when it comes to the possibility of Communion for divorced Catholics who remarry outside the Church?

According to my mind, the Holy Father is never trying to change a doctrine or undermine some foundation of the Christian Faith. But his approach is a pastoral one — to make that teaching understandable, to discern what are the core values, the most important to announce, and what are the secondary consequences of what I would say is the most important message of Christianity. Of course, we would like everybody to be perfect, but how can we help everyone be perfect?

There was some discussion about the therapeutic value of the holy Eucharist — that the Eucharist is not a reward for those who are perfect but a medicine for those who are weak.

But I don't think that those who are concerned about the sanctity of the
Sacrament of Matrimony are suggesting that the Eucharist is a "reward
for the perfect." They're upholding the indissolubility of marriage and
protecting the sacredness of the Eucharist. After all, Saint Paul said, "For
anyone who eats and drinks without discerning the body, eats and drinks
judgment on himself" (1 Cor 11:29). And they're trying to defend that
against what they perceive as a threat to that doctrine.

I don't think that doctrine is threatened at all. Even more, that doctrine,
through the pastoral approach of the Holy Father, is proclaimed. So, let's
make this discernment, but let's recognize that we need God's forgiveness, we need God's mercy, and we need the Body and Blood of Christ in
order to reach salvation. We cannot be saved only because of our good
and adequate behavior. We can fulfill the divine commandments only by
the power of the Holy Spirit.

Of course, there is an invitation to conversion. We have to be converted and believe in the Gospel. It's why the Holy Father so constantly calls
for penance. If we listen carefully, constantly he speaks of penance. But
very often people today don't understand what it means to do penance.
And the Sacrament of Confession is at the heart of Pope Francis, because
the Sacrament of Confession is a sacrament of Divine Mercy, and we
remember how on that Jubilee of Divine Mercy he established special
Missionaries of Divine Mercy — confessors with special faculties.[1]

How familiar is Pope Francis with Byzantine traditions?

I don't know, exactly. What we can understand is that he is very much
immersed in Jesuit spirituality, especially when we speak about discernment. It is very much an intellectual process, according to his point of
view. It's a way to reflect. I remember the methodology of the Synod [on
Youth, the Faith, and Vocational Discernment] was *Listen, Reflect, and Act.*

I would say that is pretty much the way to act according to Saint Ig-
natius, which is very interesting, because previously we would consider a
doctrine, then we would try to make a good catechism, and according to

---

1. To pardon even sins that are normally reserved to the Holy See.

that, act. It has its own reasonable value.

But the pope proposed a different approach. He said the reality is more important than your ideas. So we have to listen to consider reality, then reflect, which means in the light of the Christian Faith, of the word of God, of the doctrine, make a discernment, because reflection means "evaluate according to some criteria." And then act, and your action can be sufficient, adequate for that moment, and understandable by the people, more human and so on.

So, I would find his way to approach is more of a Jesuit one. That doesn't mean it's against the Byzantine tradition at all. But the accents are very Western.

Would you say Francis's interest in synodality is different from his predecessors? Is he influenced by the Eastern concept of synodality at all?

Well, we have to be very careful using those terms, because they can mean different things. According to the synodality of the Eastern tradition, synod includes only bishops, and synodality means making decisions together with brother bishops who receive a grace of the Sacrament of Orders as successor to the apostles. The bigger body of participation we would call the Patriarchal Council, a council of the local Church. So that gathering would include representatives of the laity, of religious life, priests, and bishops. And they would reflect on specific issues.

In the Orthodox tradition, that council also very often has a legislative power. That council of the local Church can elect a primate of the Church. But according to the Canon Law of the Eastern Catholic Churches, that council has only advisory power. So that council makes resolutions, like advice, to the Synod of Bishops. And bishops in the synod discuss those proposals, that advice, and vote. The Patriarch would promote those decisions, and only then would they become obligatory, mandatory for everyone.

So, there are different steps toward the final decision.

In the Roman Catholic tradition, there is a different policy. The Synod of Bishops, which the pope convokes, by its nature is an advisory body. So, the final document of that synod is like a suggestion to the Holy

Father. It's only after the pope takes that final document and takes into consideration those suggestions that he prepares a post-synodal letter. And that letter becomes like an expression of the Magisterium of the Church, even if at the synod bishops and other participants vote for each paragraph of the final document.

The same way, synodality includes a possibility for the laity, especially in the synodality of the local church. But even the bishops' conferences cannot make final decisions. They can discuss pastoral issues and coordinate action. But who makes the decision? The local bishop.

So, there are two different traditions and two different ideas about how to have the people of God participate in the decision-making. But always there is some specific authority to make a final decision. It's important to have a space to listen. It's important to listen to good advisors. It's important to pay attention to the proposal of the council. But who makes the decision is the question.

Is Francis's interest in pursuing the restoration of communion with the Orthodox Churches different from his predecessors in any way?

My opinion is that he is in continuity with his predecessors. John Paul II made that goal not to create a worldwide jurisdiction of the pope over Orthodox communities but to restore the communion, because the biggest sign of Church unity is not the unified canon law which binds everybody, but communion, expressed by the concelebration, participation in the same Eucharistic celebration, a possibility to communicate the same Body and Blood of Christ which we consecrate together as an expression of the unity of the body of the Church. We can have different traditions. We can express the mystery of the Christian Faith in different ways. The most important thing is that the universality, the catholicity of the Church is preserved.

According to that vision, John Paul II, in his outstanding encyclical *Ut Unum Sint*, asked for help: "Please help me understand what I can do, as a successor of Peter," because we as Catholics believe that the successor of Peter in his very unique charism has received from Christ a special care for universal communion — not uniformity, not universal jurisdiction, but universal communion.

But how can he pay his service to that universal communion according to the Church's situation today?

Pope Francis is trying to do the same. He is asking for help. He is trying to meet with everybody. He is trying to establish relationships. Is it sufficient? No. Is it always perfect? No. Did we achieve the final goal? No. Do we have more communion than before? No.

But do we look forward? Yes. Do we foster that desire? Yes. Should we work and pray for that unity? Yes.

In Ut Unum Sint, *John Paul asked the Orthodox to help him find a new way of exercising the primacy of the papacy that is "open to a new situation." Did he get an answer?*

I think so, because over the last decade we can witness very interesting work of the Joint Orthodox-Catholic Theological Commission, which is discussing that issue: synodality and primacy. And there *is* some progress — very interesting progress. It is a movement toward each other. Orthodox started from the grassroots level. They considered, "OK, there is a need for communion of the local community with the local bishop. Then there is need for communion of the bishops with their primate." Now they are discussing the need for universal communion, as we witnessed those efforts to call a Pan-Orthodox Council in Crete.[2] Some Orthodox (for example, the Moscow Patriarchate) would deny any reasons for the very existence of the universal authority in the Church of Christ, even if that authority is expressed by the ecumenical councils in our days. They are questioning even a possibility to convoke such an ecumenical council for Orthodoxy today. *So, we will meet together, we will decide together, and then the local primates of our Churches are obliged to fulfill our decision.* Some of them will deny that: *There is no kind of universal jurisdiction, even the common decision of all the patriarchs that would be imposed on me to make my decision for my own Church.*

But there is a movement toward discussion of consideration for the need for universal authority.

---

2. A gathering in 2016 of heads of various Orthodox Churches to promote unity.

From the Catholic perspective, Pope Francis speaks about the *sana decentralizatione* — healthy decentralization — which means that the pope is not a monarch, but there is a vision or even reevaluation of episcopal collegiality. So the pope, with the collegiality of the bishops, is ruling the Church.

So local bishops participate in the universal authority of the Holy Father. And from the Holy Father's side, there is decentralization of his duty.

So we can say that Catholics go from the top toward the grassroots level, and Orthodox from the grassroots toward the universal. But that movement is a movement to meet each other.

So, I think there *is* progress, but hopefully the Orthodox and Catholic parts will work together, because from that perspective, it shows how much we need each other. The Catholic side needs the Orthodox in order to understand the value of synodality and the collegiality of bishops, and the Orthodox need the Catholic part in order to rediscover the value and necessity in today's world of the universal authority in Christ's Church.

10

Between East and West

John Burger: For you, what does Ukrainian Greek Catholic mean? What is a Ukrainian Greek Catholic?

His Beatitude Sviatoslav: I think that our Church reflects the unity of Christ's Church of the first millennium. So that search for restoring the unity of Christ, that movement we mentioned before, we already live in our tradition. Why? Because according to our tradition, our canon law, our theological and ecclesiological vision, we are part of the Byzantine, Eastern tradition, but we recognize the unifying role of the successor of Peter, and we live our tradition in communion with him. So that meeting between East and West, between the communion from grassroots toward the universal, and that movement from the ministry of the successor of Peter toward his duty to be vigilant for the Church community worldwide is happening in the body of our Church.

So is there a special place for the Ukrainian Greek Catholic Church in the quest for restored communion between the Orthodox and Catholic Churches?

I think so, but I think we ourselves have to rediscover a message that God is giving to the universal Church through our witness today. We have to witness to the Orthodox that communion with the Holy Father doesn't mean a submission or loss of identity. The fullness of Orthodoxy will flourish inside communion with the successor of Peter. We ourselves have not only to rediscover but make flourish, manifest in its fullness the Byzantine tradition, which is common for us and the Orthodox. And on the other hand, the successor of Peter, with his collaborators in the Roman Curia, [has] to show through the relations toward us how [he] would like to treat the Orthodox, when one day they will restore communion with the successor of Peter.

So, there is a special mission of the Eastern Catholics in the Church of Christ today for the restoration of full communion. It is why we would say the ecumenical mission of each Eastern Catholic Church, the ecumenical mission of our Church, is part of our identity. Very often, even our presence can make Orthodox and sometimes Roman Catholics feel uncomfortable. Why? Because we are like a prophecy, like a challenge, like a call for that fullness of communion, because very often, Orthodox will not care about the universality of the Church; they will be so concentrated on their local issues that the universality of the Church will become for them more theoretical than real: *Yes, we are in communion with others, but we would emphasize the local issues.*

And from the other side, Roman Catholic bishops often will be so happy in their own see that the care for the universality of the Catholic Church would be the duty only of the Holy Father. *It's his concern. We will have some relations with the Eastern Churches like some sort of exotic expression of Christian traditions, with bells and smells, but not something which really is a core value of my mission today.*

It's why we as Eastern Catholics would be teasing both sides, provoking their awareness that full communion is not reached yet. We cannot be led to the illusion that we are self-sufficient, that we do not need each other in order to manifest the fullness of the Church of Christ. The presence of our Church very often is a sign, a remembrance that we have to make a statement that today the Church of Christ is divided. And we cannot forget it. Maybe the mission of our Church is to awaken that awareness each day in respect to both sides, Catholic and Orthodox, and maybe some other perspective we can discover in time.

But it also sounds like you have some work to do in your Church to get those Byzantine traditions to flourish.

I think that the renewal of our Church comes through the renewal of our own roots and our own Byzantine traditions. The liturgical renewal in the Roman Catholic Church after the Second Vatican Council very often was understood as the introduction of some new rites, new traditions that never were practiced before, a new form to celebrate the sacraments. But the renewal for Eastern Catholics comes in different ways. Renewal means "reevaluate your own richness and tradition." Very often in the past, there was a special policy called *prestantia ritus Latina*, which means the supremacy of the Latin rite, the Latin tradition as the fullest expression of Catholic truth. And that policy made us feel less important. Our tradition in the fullness of the Catholic Faith was not fully expressed. And it created some sort of inferiority complex.

But renewal for us means to rediscover our own tradition, to make it vibrant, attractive in our day, and make that vibrancy of the common tradition of our Orthodox brethren present as a sign of the fruitfulness of the full communion of the Eastern Catholic Church with the successor of Peter.

So, our communion with the successor of Peter is not damaging our tradition of Eastern spirituality but gives it a new possibility to flourish.

What are your concerns about the laity in the Church?

I have to say that because of the active laity, our Church survived. That was the case in the time of the Soviet persecution. Because of our laity, we became a global Church, because of different waves of migration. Because of our laity, right now we are both a global and a local Church. Because of our laity, we are flourishing in vocations to the priesthood, monastic life, and so on. But also, the laity are very active in our parishes, in our different lay movements. Laity are the majority of the Body of Christ. We are so happy to have active lay persons who are so aware of their own responsibility for the future of their Church.

How do you see the work of the Ukrainian Greek Catholic Church in the United States right now?

I think our Church in the USA has to experience its renewal, its spring, because on the one hand, we have to maintain our tradition, maintain our roots, but on the other hand, we have to be a missionary Church. We have to be open to everybody in the USA. We are a Ukrainian Church, but we are a Church not only for Ukrainians.

On the one hand, we have to deeply appreciate and incarnate our tradition, our spiritual treasure in our communities. On the other hand, we have to be open enough to share that treasure of the Incarnation of the word of God in the body of our Church in our nation with everybody. We have to maintain the Ukrainian tradition and language, but we have to eloquently speak English and be able to help the sons and daughters of other nations who live in the USA to fall in love with our traditions.

Have you noticed good examples there that can be emulated?

Yes, there are a lot of good examples, a lot of vibrant parishes. But I think that our Church has to bring those examples to prominence in order that others can imitate them.

I think the challenge of our Church in the United States also is a very fast migration inside the country, because very often, the Ukrainian community will build a church, build a community, but within ten years, everybody will have moved to another state. What should be done with that church? How can we detect our new presence and accompany our people, to follow them to new places in the USA? How to be more dynamic?

It's a challenge, and we have no universal answers.

What does your Church and your tradition have to offer the broader culture in North America and the universal Church, primarily the dominant Latin Catholic Church?

Well, I'm convinced we have much to share. First of all, the experience of our martyrdom, the experience that the Church, which is small and persecuted, can be strong and vibrant; the Church which is authentic is more important than the Church of big numbers. And many other things, because I'm convinced that vibrancy and authenticity of Church life make the Church authentic and attractive, even in the situation of a country like the USA. Maybe our experience can be interesting even to the Roman Catholic Church. But we have to be open, vibrant, and well integrated into the Catholic Church as such in the USA.

I think an important way to share our tradition is to be present in the intellectual world. I'm so pleased that at The Catholic University of America in Washington, a special department for Eastern Christian studies has been established.[1] Without a vibrant and important intellectual center, it is not possible to be comprehensive; it is almost impossible to have enough possibilities to communicate with the world.

Some Christians in the West are discovering the "Light of the East," to quote a title of a letter by Pope John Paul II.[2] Some Roman Catholics have been known to embrace Eastern traditions. But does it work in reverse? Are there elements of Western spirituality that you find attractive, that members of your Church find attractive? What about the Rosary, Eucharistic adoration, devotion to Saint Joseph?

I have to say that maybe, according to the vision of my predecessor, Lubomyr Husar, the mission of our Church is to be a mediator between East and West — Eastern tradition and Western Christian tradition. But I think even in today's globalized world, we are very much isolated from each other. We are too self-centered. We already mentioned that even if free access to the source and foundation of the Christian Faith is increas-

---

1. The Institute for the Study of Eastern Christianity.

2. Pope St. John Paul II, *Orientale Lumen* ("The Light of the East"), May 2, 1995, vatican.va.

ing, there is also increasing religious ignorance. There is also an increase of ignorance between Eastern and Western Christians. Catholics of the Western tradition know less and less about Eastern Catholics, and I have to say that Eastern Catholics or Orthodox know almost nothing about Roman Catholics.

Aside from Latinizations that had been forced on Eastern Catholics in North America in the past.

Yes, but real communion means the interchange of experiences. So, I think we have to be aware that that communion means interaction and knowledge and the possibility to overcome some prejudices against each other. We do still have those. And I hope that one day we will be able, without any prejudice or fear, to share the best examples of the pastoral care, intellectual achievements, and piety, according to each other's traditions.

Your predecessor, His Beatitude Lubomyr, invited the Knights of Columbus to Ukraine, and you have supported the growth of the Knights here. The Knights of Columbus was founded by a Latin Catholic priest, Bl. Michael J. McGivney, and in many ways, they seem to be more at home in the West than in Eastern Churches. Do you ever worry that their influence might clash with or detract from the Byzantine nature of your Church? Are there ways this Catholic fraternal order needs to be adapted to Eastern Catholicism?

The experience of the Knights of Columbus in Ukraine might be just the opposite. The Knights in Ukraine are helping to rediscover the nobility of the defenders of the Christian Faith that we had in our tradition. To be a Knight means to be a noble defender: noble defender of the Christian Faith, of the Catholic Church. And the Knights right now in Ukraine are helping to rediscover those values in our own tradition.

So, we don't regard that community as a Latin one at all. It is why the most dynamically growing communities in Ukraine are among the Byzantine Catholics, maybe because we are a bigger Church than the Roman Catholic Church in Ukraine. But on the other hand, those values — charity, fraternity, the defense of the Christian Faith, family values — they are so understandable and they are so needed that the communities that help you to foster those values are becoming more and more attractive.

And I have to say that the Knights in Ukraine right now are very attractive for most active members of our laity and organize more prominent people in Ukraine — the highest level of Ukrainian intellectual and social society. And I am so thankful because the experience of the Knights from the United States helped us rediscover our own traditions even more, bringing that tradition to the international level.

So, there is some incarnation of the charism of Father McGivney in Ukraine's situation, but also sharing of Ukrainian tradition and history with the worldwide community of the Knights of Columbus.

And we both benefit.

Several of your predecessors have been cardinals of the Roman Catholic Church. If you were offered a red hat, how would you react? Again, it's more of a Western tradition.

Perhaps the most prominent head of the Ukrainian Greek Catholic Church of the twentieth century, Metropolitan Andrei Sheptytsky, was not a cardinal. So that dignity, that mission, that duty of the cardinal is not something which I would need in order to be a good head of the Ukrainian Greek Catholic Church.

But that is a special service to the Holy Father, assisting him in his mission. So, if one day the Holy Father asks me to assist him, well, I'll try to do my best. But it is not something I desire or need in order to be a good shepherd, a good father for my flock.

Morris West's novel **The Shoes of the Fisherman** *and the film version of it starring Anthony Quinn is the fictional story of a cardinal from a Slavic country who becomes pope. Some believe the story was loosely based on the life of your predecessor, Cardinal Josyf Slipyj. Could a Ukrainian Greek Catholic cardinal serve as Bishop of Rome? What would be different about his ministry?*

I don't know. I never think about that. Maybe your question would be a challenge for my reflection in the future. Until now, it's too hypothetical.

In February 2019, the Permanent Synod of your Church "blessed implementation of the plan of measures for the elaboration of the Charter for Charismatic Movements." So, there is a movement of the Charismatic Renewal in the Ukrainian Catholic Church? Tell me about that. Again, it's a phenomenon from Western Christianity. How do they operate within a Byzantine world?

We do have several movements which are basically coming from the Roman Catholic Church — not only in Ukraine but in the diaspora. We have the Charismatic Movement, the Neocatechumenal Way, and so on. We adopted a special attitude toward those movements. First of all, we're trying to integrate them into our ecclesial body, which means we are trying to enter into contact with them and try to help them incarnate their spirituality in our tradition. So maybe in the future, it will be some special phenomenon: a Byzantine rite charismatic movement.

But according to our pastoral policy here in Ukraine, we appointed a bishop who is in charge of the contact with the Charismatic Movement in Ukraine, because that Charismatic Movement has different communities and different schools of spirituality. So, we're trying to coordinate them, to have some sort of institutional dialogue with them, because according to their vision, the Charismatic Movement is not meant to substitute the traditional spirituality but renew it. It's why the movement is also called the "Renovation in the Holy Spirit." That's why it's vital to help incarnate that movement of the Holy Spirit inside our Church body. If not, it can create a parallel spirituality or some self-centered antagonistic communities, which can oppose themselves to existing parish communities as such. It is why we decided on the one hand to value that movement, to cherish everything good that the Holy Spirit is giving us today, but on the other hand we're trying to introduce our own people to rediscover the presence of the Holy Spirit inside our liturgical tradition.

Well, because of that, we're trying to be open to incarnate that movement, but also, we could observe those people who are involved in the

Charismatic Movement. Very often, they develop special spiritual sensitivity. They need special pastoral attention. And those groups of the Charismatic Renewal need good spiritual guidance. So we are trying to provide for them good spiritual leaders who are able to lead them into the correct path.

But also, I have to say that many people who experienced that charismatic way to approach religion discovered their vocation to consecrated or priestly life, if they were guided in the correct and mature way. So, it is why dialogue, assistance, discernment is so important in the Church's attitude toward these kinds of movements.

Charismatics have a reputation, whether deservedly or not, of being very demonstrative in their piety. You're not afraid this behavior might be misinterpreted by, say, our Orthodox brethren, who might say, "Look at those Uniates, dancing around the sanctuary or playing guitars, falling down, slain in the spirit?" Or the Neocatechumenal Way, with everyone sitting down receiving the Eucharist in their hands?

You are talking about some form of the manifestation of the Charismatic Movement. Of course, they are not according to our spiritual tradition. Sitting, dancing, receiving the holy Eucharist in the hands is something that belongs mostly in the Roman Catholic sensitivity and liturgical tradition. But we are trying to incarnate that spirit in our tradition. It is why, of course, we are careful about those chaotic spontaneous manifestations of that spirituality. We would not allow them to do that inside our celebrations.

Nevertheless, the Holy Spirit is a Person of the Divine Trinity, and is the soul of any kind of spirituality, because there is no spirituality without the Holy Spirit. Otherwise, it would be a simple human religiosity. It is why that kind of movement needs good guidance, in order to inspire from within, renew our tradition, and help our people rediscover their own tradition in light of the work of the Holy Spirit.

But I have to say also that we cannot impose that charismatic spirituality on everybody. If there are some charismatic groups in a parish, well, we will try to integrate them, but we cannot create charismatic parishes, which oblige everybody who joins that parish to practice the charismatic way of worshiping. Of course, there are special people who need more of that charismatic approach to spirituality than others. So we have to be careful to propose but not impose, be open but not be contaminated by different foreign expressions of the spirituality, be renewed by the power of the Holy Spirit but also to guide those persons in the correct way to rediscover their spiritual life as such.

You travel around the world, visiting various Ukrainian Greek Catholic eparchies and parishes. This often puts you in Roman Catholic settings. In 2018, you visited the cathedral of Naples, Italy, and had a chance to carry the famous relic of Saint Gennaro, which consists of a vial of dried blood from the fourth-century saint. While you were doing so, the blood liquefied, something that happens rather rarely and is considered to be a miracle. What are your thoughts about that? How did this happen?

It is difficult to explain. We organized a big pilgrimage of our faithful to the cathedral in Naples, commemorating the anniversary of the Ukrainian genocide — the Holodomor. It was the reason for my visit to Naples, to meet my people, but first of all to commemorate the victims of the Holodomor.

Cardinal Crescenzio Sepe of Naples received me in his cathedral with the highest expression of honor and esteem, carrying in his hands the relic of San Gennaro. It was a crowded cathedral. The most important representatives of the city council, representatives of the State of Ukraine, the ambassador of Ukraine to the Holy See, the consul general of Ukraine in Naples, priests, nuns, many Ukrainian Greek Catholic faithful from the southern part of Italy were there.

The cardinal was present in the beginning of the celebration. He brought the relic and delivered an outstanding speech. And then he exposed the relic before the altar. We celebrated Divine Liturgy, and when we finished, I was the one to carry the relic back to the chapel where it is normally kept. At the very end, almost when I was giving the relic back to the parish priest of the cathedral, it just became liquid. It was considered a miracle, because normally it would happen only for special feasts. But in the context of that celebration, commemorating that innocent blood shed by the victims of the Holodomor, the blood of the most famous martyr of Naples became liquid. It was a very touching moment.

What do you think — was it something supernatural happening there?

Well, if that solid piece of blood suddenly, in your hands, becomes liquid, and nobody can explain why, something strange is happening.

The sexual abuse crisis in the Church has been the focus of much attention in recent years, but the focus has been almost completely on the Latin Catholic Church. How has the scandal affected your Church, and what sorts of responses has the Ukrainian Greek Catholic Church made, such as better screening of seminarians?

I think that whole issue is a very sad phenomenon inside the Church, but it is with great pain that I have to affirm it is also a part of today's culture. Maybe we don't fully understand the exact causes of that phenomenon, but definitely we define that as a crime against innocent victims but also a crime against the Church of Christ. Pope Francis defines that phenomenon as the manifestation of evil, of evil in our days. Why did it happen, especially in the Church? Why did those who are supposed to witness to Christ become instruments of evil inside the Church? I have to say, we don't fully understand. It's clear that bishops in the last decades did not handle the situation well, because maybe by themselves they did not fully understand the dimensions and the depth of the evil of those crimes.

What kind of policy should we adopt? We already mentioned that when we cover evils, they increase. If we reveal and confess that evil, it will disappear, or will be annihilated. The policy that we adopted by unanimous decision of our Synod of Bishops worldwide is zero tolerance, absolute transparency, which means we will not cover up any of those sad facts. We have to pay the maximum attention and care for the victims and do everything in order to prevent such an evil behavior among the clergy.

I have to say that in our Church outside of Ukraine we were not immune to that crime. But in the situations with which I am familiar, our bishops were fully open and cooperated with civil justice. Priests were suspended and prosecuted, and victims were cared for in the best way our bishops could. Perhaps we did not discover everything. But nevertheless, there is at least a clear policy in our Church.

In Ukraine, in Soviet times, we as a Church didn't have any formal structure. We lived our Christian life as a simple community of the faithful. Thanks be to God, we didn't have any kind of declared or denounced behavior of sexual abuse within the Church structures, because they didn't exist at that time — no schools, no parishes, and the like.

But I have to say that the abuse of minors in Ukrainian society is present. It's present in families. Very often, we hear police reports that there are predators even in sports, among educators who work in the school or in orphanages, and so on. I have to say that phenomenon is present in Ukrainian society, because from the time of the Soviet Union, our society suffers different kinds of abuse of power. That kind of abuse happened very often when someone abused his authority, his confidence with children, his duties, and responsibilities.

Because of that, we do have victims of that behavior, and I have to acknowledge that very often in our formation in the seminary, in monastic communities, we do have victims of such abuse.

Seminarians were victims?

Yes, seminarians or even novices. Our problem in Ukraine is how to help them, how to treat them. Can we ordain such a person? Because we know that very often, someone who was a victim then has a tendency to become a predator.

So those are big questions, and we are trying to understand what kind of policy to adopt as a Church. I have to say that in each eparchy in Ukraine, we adopted special norms for how to treat such a case if it came to light, what kind of steps bishops should undertake according to Church law and Ukrainian law. In each diocese, we appointed persons responsible for the defense of minors in our communities, and we also adopted special norms for the pastoral care of minors.

I think we as a Church in Ukraine, thanks be to God, don't have such cases among our clergy or monastic life, but we can profit from the experience and policy of the Roman Catholic Church worldwide, to prevent, to make our communities and our schools and summer camps the safest place, where innocent children can feel safe and well-protected.

Have there been any studies or theories put forward that because of the tradition of a married priesthood, this problem might be less here than in other parts of the universal Church?

Not too much. According to our experience today, marriage or family life is not a protection against such behavior, for many reasons:

First, the majority of cases happen in families.

Second, we consider that celibacy itself is not a source of such a crime. There are some psychological causes deeply rooted in the personal behavior of the person, not a state of life — marriage or celibacy — which can provoke or prevent such behavior.

It is true that in our seminary, the majority of seminarians prepare themselves for life as married clergy, but also, they need to have good formators and good spiritual fathers in order to discern their vocation, because marriage or celibacy is a specific vocation. It's not a simple canonical status. And you have to discern your own vocation in order to make the right choice, and you need somebody to help you in that discernment, in that very important life decision.

It is also true that because of that context in the seminaries, not only the formators but the community as such is not tolerant of such deviant behavior. So, seminarians among themselves will easily detect someone who has a problem of sexual identification or his relationships with the opposite sex or minors.

So, until now, thanks be to God, we have very transparent communities, and I have to say that the issue of that kind of sex abuse is not so common in Ukrainian culture. But that doesn't mean it never happened. Maybe in the future, such cases will be revealed. But we have to be well-prepared — learning from the experience of the Western Church as well.

Do you find changing attitudes in the Vatican toward the Eastern Catholic Churches in general and the Ukrainian Church in particular?

I think there are not sudden changes, but there is increasing openness, because the Eastern Catholic Churches, especially in the Middle East, are victims of severe persecution. The Churches in Eastern Europe gave their witness to the Catholic Church during the Soviet persecution. And step by step, that martyrdom and that spiritual and liturgical tradition of the Eastern Catholic Churches is more and more rediscovered and evaluated in the West, and from the Holy See we receive a good sign of support and of accompaniment, especially [in] those situations where we are a significant minority, or we need their assistance in order to provide adequate pastoral care for our faithful.

Since the time of Cardinal Slipyj, at least, the Ukrainian Greek Catholic Church has asked Rome that it be declared a patriarchate, and yet Rome has not yet affirmed that aspiration. Why? Are you continuing to seek this status?

First of all, there is a big question whether it is possible for the Vatican to create an Eastern Catholic patriarchate as such. What is the mechanism for the creation of the Eastern Catholic patriarchates? Who is the authority that can recognize a status of patriarchate of a specific local Church?

And there is no clear answer to that question among the Orthodox, because in the past, it was the ecumenical council. Very often, Orthodox will look toward a special authority of the Ecumenical Patriarchate of Constantinople, which claims it has the right to acknowledge the autocephaly[3] for a local Church and then acknowledge their patriarchal dignity. But other Orthodox will disagree.

According to our studies, the investigation and research among our theologians, patriarchates in the East — in the Byzantine tradition, specifically — are not created but recognized. So first of all, we have to develop, to grow as a Church, and a patriarchate is a sign of full maturity and

---

3. The right of a Church to govern itself — for its patriarch not to have to report to any higher ecclesiastical authority.

capability for self-governance.

So, it's something that happens organically, and then someone has to recognize it.

Yes. It would be like: OK, you are growing. You are mature. Not because somebody recognizes it or not, but because you *are*.

So that is the case with our Church. With my predecessor, Lubomyr Husar, we adopted the policy that we have to *build* a patriarchate, not demand that somebody recognize it. We have to create, we have to develop our patriarchal way of being as a Church, with those efficient three branches: legislative, judicial, and executive. We have to be mature enough to provide adequate pastoral care for our faithful everywhere in the world. We have to be efficient in our work of evangelization. We have to be mature enough in our theological thinking. We have to be efficient in our self-governance system, which is given to us by the Code of Canons for the Eastern Catholic Churches.

So, we have to fully use the rights given us by our status as a *sui iuris* Church — a self-governing Church. And we are moving toward that goal.

So, our Church is growing, it's developing, it's exploding, becoming more and more present in a positive way everywhere in the world, participating actively in the life of the local Churches, local Roman Catholic bishops' conferences. We are more and more developing our efficiency in different cultures, in different languages, and those are the signs of our maturity. And I'm sure that sooner or later, the maturity and efficiency of that flourishing Church will be recognized.

And a patriarchate is something that you hope for, something that's important for you.

Absolutely. I have to say that we cannot say, "Well, we will not grow toward a patriarchate," because saying we will not grow means we will be dying. So, for us, the patriarchal dignity is a matter of life or death, because according to the Byzantine tradition, each local Church, according to its maturity and development, grows toward patriarchal dignity.

In the meantime, you're officially the "Major Archbishop of Kyiv-Halych."
But people refer to you as the Patriarch and address you as Your Beati-
tude. In the liturgy, you are often prayed for as the Patriarch.

I would not sign documents as a patriarch, but I cannot prohibit the people from praying for the Patriarch and working to develop our Church
toward patriarchal dignity. This is our reality.

Let's talk about the strategy the Ukrainian Catholic Church has for the
coming years.

Speaking specifically about our Church, I as head of the Church see
that it is not enough only to have a local vision for the local community.
There are different levels of how we can have a global pastoral plan for
our Church in the whole world. For the next Patriarchal Sobor, I propose three questions to reflect on, in order to be able to prepare such
a plan:

First, where are we? We are witnessing a very important change
in modern society, from a static to a very dynamic society. People are
moving around. We very often see a positive state of health of the parish if people are born, married, and die in the same parish. But today,
it's not the case anymore. Our priests around the world are saying, "We
are baptizing one person, we celebrate a marriage with another person,
and we celebrate a funeral with a very different person." We are connected because very often the people who were born and raised and
educated in a Christian way in Ukraine now are parishioners of our
parishes in California. We put much effort into the pastoral activity to
grow in the Christian life of those persons to whom we're supposed to
pass [parishioners] for the pastoral care when they move to California.

So, we have to pass them from hand to hand to another pastor in
California. It is why we need a global pastoral care, because the movements of our people are global today, and we need to know where we
are. Where are the members of our Church physically present in order
to provide for them in that place an adequate assistance?

It is why a motto of our Patriarchal Sobor will be, "Your Church is always and everywhere with you." And that is my strategy, to provide to those people an access to the pastoral care of their mother Church, according to their identities and needs.

You have also been promoting something called the Vibrant Parish program.

Ten years ago, we started this global pastoral plan called Vibrant Parish. Of course, that program will continue because it's a long-term vision. But we understand that we cannot only focus on the parish, because a parish is not an isolated reality. Parish is always part of the bigger community. We'll continue, because if our pastoral care will not reach each person, each family which is a member of the parish, our strategy will not be successful.

It's why we have to start with the very basis of the Church, which is the parish. But we also have to see the wider reality, and it is why that worldwide gathering of the delegates of each local diocesan community will help us plan our next ten years of Church pastoral activity, and we will foster our vision for the next ten years. We have to deal with this very dynamic global reality. In addition to ideas and money moving around the world, people are moving around the world. How can the Church also move? We have to be part of that movement; we have to accompany people, but we have to understand how.

In a 2011 pastoral letter, you outlined characteristics of a "vibrant parish." It is a place where the word of God is "living and active," where priest and people celebrate the sacraments faithfully and devotedly, where charity is practiced, and so forth. Can you give me an example of a parish that has impressed you in the way it is striving to be "vibrant"?

Well, I won't mention specific parishes, because we do have many vibrant parishes around the world, in different countries, in different cultural contexts, with different ethnic backgrounds.

But our vision of the vibrant parish helps us, first, to understand what *parish* mean[s] today, because when we started to prepare the pastoral plan, we understood that at that time there were five different notions of *parish*, and we were trying to concretize our various visions of the parish. And our response to that question was that a parish is a "community of communities," because it is a big challenge to modern man and woman to create community. To live in community is a big challenge. We feel that today's communities are in danger of being fragmented. *Community* is a crucial word because *community* means "unity in common." A parish is a very foundation of that unity in common, because it's a basic community [into] which each single person is supposed to be integrated.

But we also have big parishes, and it is almost impossible to create a community when a parish has three thousand, four thousand, or five thousand persons. It is more or less possible to create a community with one heart and one soul when it is a small parish. But also, a small parish can be synonymous with a weak parish — a parish that needs a special pastoral care offered by its bishop.

So, the key word at this level is *vibrant* community.

In January 2019, we witnessed a historic event in which the Ecumenical Patriarch of Constantinople, Bartholomew I, granted a tomos of autocephaly to the Orthodox Church of Ukraine. You made a statement at that time in which you expressed your desire for Catholics and Orthodox to be part of "one Kyivan Patriarchate." What did you mean by that?

First of all, we really are happy for the development of the Orthodox Church of Ukraine as an independent, autocephalous Church. The ecumenical mission is part of the identity of each Eastern Catholic Church, and in our ecumenical engagement, it was very important to understand who our counterpart is. To whom are we supposed to direct our message of unity? Before, the Moscow Patriarchate was the only one who claimed the absolute right to speak on behalf of the Ukrainian Orthodox, and to develop that kind of dialogue with Moscow, with the center outside of Ukraine, was very difficult.

So now we hope that the newborn and newly recognized Ukrainian autocephalous Church will be engaged in the ecumenical movement as such. And we will consider — recognized by Orthodoxy worldwide — the autocephalous Ukrainian Church our privileged interlocutor to develop such a dialogue.

Of course, the ecumenical dialogue means not only friendly relations with someone who is different, but ecumenical dialogue means to look for some way to reestablish Christian unity. So always, ecumenism is a search for the possibilities of how to become united.

Here in Ukraine, we understand that that Orthodox Church needs time to grow and strengthen. That Church needs time to enter into communion with other Orthodox Churches worldwide. But also, we are aware, if we look forward, if Orthodox and Catholics find a path to unity, with whom are we supposed to be prepared to create our unity? With the Orthodox in Ukraine. Because we are in Ukraine, it is weird to speak about unity with the Orthodox in Russia. Or Orthodox in Constantinople — because we are in Ukraine. That is our territory. That is our homeland. And that is the space to look for Christian unity, specifically.

So that is why, in my opinion right now, we have a very similar situation as it was in the first part of the seventeenth century, when in Ukraine, which at that time belonged to the Polish-Lithuanian State, there was Kyivan Christianity presented in two expressions: Orthodox and Catholic. And at that time the metropolitan of the Orthodox Church was Petro Mohyla. The metropolitan of the Kyivan Church in union with Rome was Metropolitan Josyf Veliamyn Rutski. And those two prominent holy men were looking together for a way to overcome that division, and the model they were considering was the joint common patriarchate in Kyiv, which can be the space of restored unity between the Orthodox and Catholic parts of that divided Church of Kyiv, which in the first millennium was united.

So, it was a reason for my proposal, a reason for my extended hand to our Orthodox brethren. Will we have that chance in our days? We will see. How long will we have to wait for Christian unity between Orthodox and Catholics? We will see.

The Church has been divided for more time than it's been united. Restoration of communion almost seems like an impossible dream.

Yes, but on the other hand — especially in the second part of the twentieth century — the ecumenical movement is not a matter of dreaming or theoretical research; it's a matter of fact inherent to the Church life in our days. So, I consider that that authentic movement in the body of the Church of Christ is a motion of the Holy Spirit. The restoration of the unity of the Church is also a work of the Holy Spirit, but also a prayer of our Lord Jesus Christ.

So, it is not only merely a human thing, but it is also a divine work. It is why we pray for Christian unity. We work — I mean, we cooperate with the Holy Spirit — for the sake of restoring Christian unity.

And of course, we're trying to understand how we can do it in the circumstances of the historical period of the existence of the Church we are in charge of.

In the impasse that seems to be blocking full Catholic-Orthodox communion, are people on both sides clinging to certain things, refusing to give up certain positions?

Well, I have to say that at the grassroots level, simple believers are further ahead in the ecumenical movement than the monastic communities or clergy. In Ukraine today, there is a special demand of Ukrainian society for Christian unity, and I think that kind of expectation, that demand, which comes from the simple people, is a challenge, a vocation, and some sort of project which we as clergy, as leaders of those Churches, should detect, understand, and obey, and to go forward in that way.

Now we agree in Ukraine that Catholics and Orthodox have to work together on behalf of the common good of the Ukrainian nation. Working together on behalf of the common good means to be united in action. Maybe that unity in action, unity in serving the same common good, will be the first step to restore the inner unity among us.

Have you begun to work with Metropolitan Epiphanius of the Orthodox

Church of Ukraine, or have your two churches begun anything concrete in working together?

There are several fields where we already work together, even before the tomos of autocephaly was granted: assisting refugees, helping those who are victims of the Russian aggression,[4] the military chaplaincy. Those are examples of concrete actions which we spontaneously, without any hesitation, undertake. What kind of second steps should we take? We will see.

But we as the Ukrainian Greek Catholic Church have to respect the inner dynamism of the Ukrainian Orthodox Church. As I mentioned, they are mostly focused on restoring unity among the Orthodox. And I think that is the first and most important path toward Christian unity, because when Orthodox among themselves are divided, it is very complicated to project any kind of common work or efficient relations between Orthodox and Catholics.

So right now, they are focused on overcoming divisions among other Orthodox and also entering into communion with global Orthodoxy. And I think that we have to respect their priorities, to have a gentle and patient way for them, but also to pray for them and support in different ways as we can right now, to educate our people to be friendly and open to our Orthodox brethren, to form an awareness that the future of Ukraine depends on the common cooperation and common service of both sides for the sake of the common good of our state.

So, Ukraine as a common project unites us. And then we will see. We will ask for the guidance of the Holy Spirit and his illumination.

---

4. In the east of Ukraine and Crimea. The answer was provided before the more widespread Russian invasion of 2022.

11

The Revolution

John Burger: You spoke of waves of migration. What will be the conse-quences for Ukraine and for your Church of the new wave of migration that began in recent times?[1]

His Beatitude Sviatoslav: Right now, we don't fully understand the phe-nomenon of new emigration, first of all, because we live in a world that is not static but very dynamic. The world is becoming a small village, and the speed of movement is increasing, not only the movement of ideas, the style of life, music, and the way to use different material things, but also the speed of movement of the people. And I think that maybe in the near future, any obstacles to prevent travel and movement across borders will be less and less relevant. So that globalization will make us feel like citizens of the world.

But the phenomenon of emigration from Ukraine is also marked by

---

1. This question was asked in 2019, almost three years before the Russian invasion of Ukraine led to a massive number of refugees leaving the country.

the Russian aggression; so many people in the east of Ukraine had to flee from their homes because of military action. But very often, they simply changed their place inside Ukraine, so we have an inner migration. But also, many people from throughout Ukraine are going to find a new homeland outside of Ukraine, and it has positive and negative effects. Ukraine is losing the best part of its youth, the best part of its society, the people of the middle class, well-educated, good businessmen, who are looking for better conditions to realize their gifts, to be safer, more protected, have more possibilities to achieve their goals.

And who will stay to develop our country? Who will work? Who will develop our economy? What kinds of politicians will we have in the future? Those are concerns.

But on the other hand, we see that the globalization of the Ukrainian world is coming. Those who are leaving Ukraine bring Ukraine with them. They establish new Ukrainian communities. They are asking for pastoral care. So, our priests are following them, and we are establishing new parishes. Maybe in the future there will be new eparchies, new metropolises. So, through that migration, the globalization of our Church is still taking place.

That globalization is not something that is simply a matter of the past but is also a matter of our future. But the whole issue is how to help them maintain their identity, how to establish relations between Ukraine, between the head of the Church and that big and dynamic diaspora. How to interact? And we can see that those who live in the diaspora are involved in the development of society in Ukraine. They very often bring to Ukraine new experience, new vision. Maybe in the future, they will have the possibility to maintain their citizenship and participate in the public life of Ukraine, even if they are living in a different part of the world. So there is a whole renewal of the system of participation in the state life; there is a big transformation of Ukrainian society on different levels, but also it is a big challenge for the Church, for the global Ukrainian Church community, but also for the Ukrainian Church in Ukraine.

Perhaps we discover our weaknesses very often through the diaspora. We started to realize how inefficient the catechetical service is, because very often those who go outside of Ukraine show a very low knowledge of their Faith. So that new emigration is like a mirror in which we can look and consider the efficiency of our pastoral work in Ukraine.

So that is a whole new phenomenon that we are trying to study, understand, and comprehend, and we are trying to find an adequate response.

Why should Ukraine matter to the rest of the world?

I think that the current situation in Ukraine [in 2019] demonstrates that we are working on issues that are very important for the rest of the world.

The first we mentioned is an ecumenical one, and I think that Ukraine is, according to the expression of Pope St. John Paul II, a laboratory of ecumenism. Divisions among the Orthodox can divide global Orthodoxy, but the solution and the way to overcome that division can help global Orthodoxy find a path for unity and redefine universal authority.

Second, Russian aggression against Ukraine is not a Ukrainian war; it's a global conflict. Why? Because Ukraine is only the context, where the whole international security system is falling apart. If a bigger and stronger state can simply attack a smaller one, it means that the global security system is under threat. If we have a case where the law of a stronger, more powerful state is becoming more important than the power of the law, it means that the entire world is under threat.

Third, in the very beginning of its independence from the Soviet Union, Ukraine was a state in possession of nuclear weapons. In order to give an example for the disposition of nuclear arms on the global level, Ukraine agreed to give up those arms. But Ukraine as a state asked for guarantees from the international community, and such guarantees — the so-called Budapest Memorandum of 1994, which was signed by Ukraine, Russia, the United States, Great Britain, and other countries — [were] the case when one small state decided to give up their nuclear arms in exchange for the guarantee of the international system of security.

Well, now, when those guarantees are practically destroyed,[2] who in the world will believe in nuclear disarmament? Who in today's world will rely on international guarantees of security? And that can lead to escalation in the relationships between states, and the situation of the Cold War can once again become a reality.

Fourth, the war against Ukraine since 2014 has been called a "hybrid war," waged not only with arms but also with the economy and with disinformation. So if money in today's world becomes more important than human life, it will be the end of democracy — not only in Russia but everywhere in the world, because citizens in Germany and the United States will have no trust in their government, because they will feel they are simply a matter for negotiation. Their lives are worth nothing. Maybe a barrel of oil is more important than the life of human beings.

Disinformation is something that is part of today's world. Some philosophers say we are living today in a post-truth culture. Well, if there is no objective truth anymore, it means I cannot trust anybody. I cannot trust the information I receive from the media. I cannot trust the promises of our politicians. And we can see how the dangers of populism are increasing in the world.

So that lack of credibility will destroy everything — nations, states from within, the economy, and worldwide system of relationships, on different levels: political, economic, even military.

So all those issues right now are concentrated in Ukraine. It is why I'm convinced there's no military solution for the crisis in Ukraine. I'm convinced that the war in Ukraine is not a simple Ukrainian issue; it's a global conflict. And the whole international community has to undertake its own responsibility to prevent a collapse of the whole network of relations which make us citizens of the same world.

Even the process of globalization brings us to the realization that everything happening in one part of the world immediately affects all of us. So, the war in Ukraine is not only about us here on Ukrainian territory, but it is also about you, everywhere in the world: USA, Great

---

2. Because there were practically no consequences for Russia's occupation of Crimea and the Russia-backed separatist movement in Eastern Ukraine.

Britain, Europe, Latin America, Australia, and the rest of the world.

At the same time, here in Ukraine you have a society that was radically transformed by decades of living under communism. You're trying to get beyond that, to bring man back to his true nature after years of the project of the "New Soviet man." How does the situation play into the scenario you describe?

Maybe because of the Soviet past, those signs of transformation are so evident in Ukraine — more evident than elsewhere in the world. The Soviet Union was the biggest experiment in how to manipulate not only history, not only religion, but also the human being. The goal of Soviet propaganda was to form the Soviet human person — *Homo Sovieticus*. It was especially programmed to destroy the identity of particular nations which were in the territory of the Soviet Union and create a unified Soviet nation.

It is true that the quick transformation after the fall of the Soviet Union for us was very traumatic, because from a post-Soviet country we quickly had to be able to establish a very efficient modern democracy. We had to realize in everyday life the European values — those values which very often in Europe are forgotten or neglected. So, all those circumstances in the past made the transformation in Ukraine more evident and dramatic.

But it indicates that Ukraine in some way is in the same condition as the whole world today. And those issues which are so crucial for Ukraine right now in its inner reality are the issues that are so important for the future of the world, and we are asking the international community: "Don't give up on Ukraine. Don't leave us alone. Because if you leave us alone, it simply means that you are running away from the solution of your own problems. So, let's do that not-so-easy job together, and only in that case can we be successful and together can build a better world for future generations."

In what ways is the Church reevangelizing Ukraine in the wake of the Soviet experience?

I have to say that after the fall of the Soviet Union, when the first signs of religious freedom in Ukraine appeared, we saw a big revival of religious life. Our Church came forth from the catacombs. The Ukrainian Orthodox were trying to break with Moscow and to establish a national Church. We experienced a huge development of the Protestant communities. The reestablishment of the Jewish communities included the rebuilding of synagogues all over Ukraine. Our Muslim brothers began to freely manifest their religious identity. And you can imagine in many cities of Ukraine, mosques started to be built.

But of course, after the period of persecution and annihilation of any kind of manifestation of religious life, those first moments of freedom were also [moments] of tension between churches. But thanks be to God, and because of a good spirit of the leaders of the churches, at the end of the 1990s, we enjoyed a period of religious peace and very good religious cooperation between the churches. In Ukraine, an outstanding organization was established, which the chief rabbi of Ukraine, Yaakov Dov Bleich, who was born in New York, has called the most powerful NGO in Ukraine. It's called the All-Ukrainian Council of Churches and Religious Organizations, and it represents 95 percent of religious life in Ukraine. And if we think of how many people consider how important religious life is for them, that council represents 75 percent of the citizens of Ukraine. This organization is a very good platform for all of us — to meet, to stay together, to cooperate for the good of the Ukrainian nation. It is how we attained religious peace in Ukraine, and how today all religious organizations in Ukraine are united on behalf of maintaining Ukrainian independence, religious freedom, and the democracy of Ukraine as an independent European country.

But I have to say, when I was a professor of moral theology, I used to teach my students that the social teaching of the Church is a very effective and important instrument in the evangelization of society. I used to repeat that phrase over and over again. But at that time, when I was a professor, I did not fully understand what I was saying. Now I have my own experience: The Good News, the Gospel of Jesus Christ is supposed to be mediated through the service of the Church in order to enlighten people's concrete human situations in light of the Gospel. If we preach about the love of God but we don't defend the dignity of the human person as the first cornerstone of the social teaching of the Church, no one will understand *why God loves me. Who am I that he should love me?* And after the Soviet system of annihilation of human dignity, the affirmation and defense of human dignity was the first task of the Church in her work of evangelization: to be human, to defend the dignity of each citizen, regardless of his religious, ethnic, or political background. If we want to build a free and independent country, create a society where each individual will have enough of a possibility to realize himself, we have to rethink the whole system of how our society works.

Second, in the Soviet era, the importance of the collective was emphasized, the importance of the group. According to the state programs, it was a program of collectivization. So you were deprived of all your personal belongings, especially in the villages, and all land, all animals, all beans were supposed to be common for everybody. This emphasis of the common in the post-Soviet society led to an opposite effect: Everybody was thinking only about his own deal, so that collectivization in the past provoked some sort of an extreme individualism.

So, in the early 1990s, we were living like a wild capitalism. In those conditions, we as a Church were supposed to emphasize the importance of community, and the second principle of the social teaching of the Church, the common good, was so important. The common good means the very foundation of the state; it means a final goal of each politician, who is supposed to be elected in order to serve the common good of everyone.

But I have to say that in today's individualistic culture, the whole idea of the common good is very difficult to preach, because everybody thinks about only his own business.

So the third cornerstone of the Church's social teaching, which is vital for evangelization of society, is solidarity. The so-called Revolution of Dignity, which we lived through in 2014, was an expression of outstanding solidarity of the Ukrainian people. Solidarity because of the defense of human dignity — the very name of the Revolution of Dignity reflected this — and common good, because people were united in the defense of Ukraine as a state, its integrity, as a common good. Suddenly, that solidarity enabled Ukrainian society to give an adequate response to a huge humanitarian catastrophe, which is going on right now in Ukraine. In only a few months, we started to have millions of internally displaced persons, when the Russian aggression started, when the Russian Army entered Ukrainian territory.[3] So people had to leave behind all their belongings and leave the place they lived.

When millions of Syrian refugees entered Germany [in 2015], that powerful state started to experience severe problems. But the economy of Ukraine — we cannot compare it with the economy of Germany — was able to receive millions of [internal] refugees. Why wasn't a weak Ukrainian state destroyed because of this internal displacement? Because of the solidarity of Ukrainians.

In many villages of Central and Western Ukraine, when those displaced persons would come to the supermarket asking for groceries, there was a sheet of paper on which those people could list the product they received. And people in the villages would come and pay for those groceries. It's just a small example. It was just spontaneous. Nobody asked, "Who are you? What language do you speak? To which church do you go?" Only, "Because you are in need, I will help you."

So when we promote solidarity as part of the Gospel of Jesus Christ in such circumstances, you can see it being put into action among the people.

And the fourth cornerstone, I would say even a key to building a successful, free, and democratic society, is the principle of subsidiarity, private initiative. [I] will not wait until somebody comes and defends my country. It is my duty. [I] will not expect that the rich Western countries come and rebuild my house, my city. No, I have to do that. It's my responsibility. So people finally felt responsible for their state, for their country, for the future of their children. And that was exactly the opposite of what was happening in the Soviet Union, because government was responsible for everything.

I remember a situation in the Soviet Army where an officer called a poor soldier in front of the unit and started to yell at him. And he tried to justify himself by saying, "Well, but I thought that …" and the officer stopped him: "You have no right to think. You have only to faithfully

---

3. Referring to the Russian annexation of Crimea in February 2014.

and on time execute my orders." And people were afraid in post-Soviet Ukraine to undertake private initiatives. Even in the seminary, it was not so easy to educate our seminarians to have their private initiatives. Why? Because if you are quiet and simply follow orders, no one can punish you because of your mistakes. So you are very good with authorities but have no initiatives. To have initiatives was a way to defend yourself against an oppressive system. But we have to educate people to be free. Freedom is not only an absence of external coercion; freedom is a spiritual category: the inner freedom. Only truth and God's grace can set us free.

This is just a small example of how those four basic principles of the social teaching of the Church — human dignity, common good, solidarity, and subsidiarity — in today's circumstances, for us, [are] a pastoral key [for] how to evangelize Ukrainian society.

But what can the Church be doing to help people better understand the truth of the Gospel when they have no interest in religion at all, or they think they don't?

Well, I have no simple answer to that, because there are different, very important levels to that problem that we have to be aware of. But let me mention one that I think is very important, and we lived that reality in the Soviet Union, which was mostly an atheistic country — a country of Nones.

Very often, we will declare ourselves to be no part of a community because of our comprehension of that community — that church, that religion — very often because of our prejudice or bad experience. So very often, I would define myself as a None according to my own imagination. And that personal opinion, personal view, personal imagination in the world of increasing individualism is getting more and more predominant. And very often, I'm dealing not with the authentic Church, religion, or even persons, but with my own prejudice, with my own imagination, or my own personal experience, which is always a segmented one, because I experienced something with someone in certain circumstances in some part of the Church or parish — my personal contact with a religious group.

Second, among those who are still Christian or Catholic, according to the opinion of Pope Benedict XVI, their religious ignorance is increasing. So if I tell someone I'm a Christian, very often, I have no idea what I'm saying. So, very often, I myself present to someone as a Catholic giving a bad image or bad example or bad witness to what the Catholic Church is all about. So I give an impression, and in his opinion a wrong vision, of the Catholic Church. Or worse, if I commit a crime, that destroys the good name of my Church.

Thirdly, in the world of fake news and post-*veritas*, a Christian witness is very important. I think that in order to give a Christian witness to those who are Nones, we have to be authentic, we have to not only speak up or speak about but to make some symbolic actions and gestures, and to be aware that the Catholic Church is also me, as a part of that reality. So in order to be able to represent an authentic face of my Church, I have to learn more about my Faith.

Very often in the post-communist society, we understood that many people believed in God but did not know him. And we found that our duty was to help them know the God they believe in. I am convinced that each person in this world, maybe in different ways, believes — believes in some positive success of his good action, believes that good can be real, and ultimately, they do believe in God, but according to their own imagination about him.

So there is some religious identity of each person, but we as Christians today have to help those Nones who believe in that God to know him.

In 2004, you went to the Maidan, the central square of Kyiv, for the Orange Revolution. You were a priest. In 2013–2014, you went back for the Revolution of Dignity, now as an archbishop and head of the Ukrainian Greek Catholic Church. How often did you go to the protests, and what did you do there? Did you pray with people, counsel people, tend to the wounded or dying?

First of all, I have to say that Maidan was a sudden eruption of a very strong and active civil society in Ukraine. We mentioned that Ukrainian society is a post-communist country in a very dynamic transformation. Twenty-five years ago, many analysts were discussing whether civil society in post-Soviet countries existed at all. Why? Because in the Soviet Union, they were all controlled by the state, and this made the development of civil society impossible. But the eruption of the Maidan protests showed that in Ukraine such a society really exists, is very dynamic, and is becoming the main actor of the transformation of our country.

I have to say that no politicians, no churches, were able to provoke such a phenomenon. It was a spontaneous reaction of the simple people from different backgrounds — religious, ethnic origin — against the oppressive, corrupt, unjust government. People suddenly just said, "Never again will we tolerate violence against our children or youth."

Second: In such circumstances, the post-Soviet society was dynamically developing a civil society. Where is the place of the Church? Especially, where is the place of the community of the Catholic Church?

According to the social doctrine of the Church and our own historical tradition, the Ukrainian Greek Catholic Church never was a Church of the state. It was always a Church of the simple people. And we understood the Church in Ukraine as an integral part of civil society, not of the state system, not of business, but of civil society, because who are we? We are simple but active citizens who are oriented according to special values — in our case, Christian values. So, if we are part of civil society, and that civil society is standing in the middle of the central square — the Maidan — in Kyiv, where is our place? Where are we supposed to be? We're supposed to be there, with our people. And people in Maidan were asking Church leaders to be with them and to pray with them. And religious life, constant prayer — led by representatives of different religions — was a part of that reality. Even when the most dramatic events started in Maidan, you could see young men and women making a line for confession and then go[ing] to the barricades. And very often after that confession, they were killed. How many people were baptized at Maidan!

I remember the observation of the Lutheran pastor — because the Lutheran church is right near the presidential administration building, in the central part of Kyiv. And it was a very cold period of winter, and many protesters, including the wounded, found shelter in that church. And I was visiting those places where the victims were gathered — the so-called underground hospitals. And I went to that Lutheran church. The majority of those people were Greek Catholics. And when I finished my visit, I approached the pastor — he was a German citizen — to thank him. And he told me, "Your Beatitude, you do not need to thank me at all. Do you know why? Because this is not a simple people standing in the center of Kyiv. Christ is standing with them. And we simply are doing our duty. We serve Christ."

I was impressed, because he was almost like a detached onlooker. For him, it would have been a lot easier and safer to close his church and say, "It is not my duty or interest." But he acted differently, and his service was authentic *diakonia*. And through his spiritual understanding, I realized that our service to those wounded people, the veneration of the wounds of those people in reality is the veneration of the wounds of the body of Christ.

Maidan also was a very specific moment when post-Soviet society opened its doors to evangelization.

How so?

Because people were asking for the presence of the ministers of different Christian churches. People were sensitive to the message of the Gospel. Maybe several years earlier, the majority of them were not sensitive to Church issues. At that moment, we Orthodox, Catholics, and Protestants realized: "If we do not cross that opened door, maybe in the future, that door will be closed. The word of God, the Church, will no longer be a part of the life of those people, a part of the life of Ukrainian society." But we had to have enough courage, enough sensitivity to the signs of the times, as the Second Vatican Council put it, to be there, to say and announce the right words at the right moment in the right place. And I have to say that the majority of Ukrainian society rediscovered the role of the Church, thanks to those dramatic circumstances.

After people began to get seriously injured, even killed, did you try to play any kind of role as a mediator or intervene with government officials?

We members of the Council of Churches and Religious Organizations were trying to mediate between protesters and the government in order to prevent violence. We were protecting those people almost for two months, but at some point, we did not succeed anymore. There was an eruption of violence. It was difficult to detect who started first, but in that case, we were trying to stop the violence, but without success. So we started to assist those who were wounded.

And you asked about the Knights of Columbus. The Knights were taking away from the city in their own cars hundreds of persons, saving their lives, because the government [of Russia-friendly Viktor Yanukovych] issued special laws. They were looking in the hospitals in Kyiv for people who were wounded on the street in order to put them in jail. We witnessed many cases of people who would jump from the second or third floor windows in order to flee from the police who were coming to the hospital to arrest them. It is why we started to open the underground hospitals, but we were not able to provide all kinds of medical care. So we were trying to take them out of the city in order to put them in the state hospitals in other cities. The Knights of Columbus took those people, with the bloodshed, in their own cars, at their own risk, to hospitals outside the city, and they saved hundreds of lives.

Is the Revolution of Dignity ongoing?

I think so. Perhaps it is taking different expressions and forms. Immediately after Maidan, many people from Kyiv went to Donbas to stop the invasion of the Russian Army, even if they were without arms. Many of them were killed in the first two weeks of that battle. People throughout the country were collecting money in order to buy them bulletproof vests and other protection. And basically, they stopped that invasion, even without arms. That was a different form of Maidan.

But also, another form of the Revolution of Dignity is pressure of society on the reforms of the state system, the healthcare system, the system of justice in Ukraine, the very administration of the president's office, and so on. So there is constant pressure and vigilance of civil society over the functioning of the Ukrainian state.

The next one is the openness of Ukrainian society and transparency — even with some extremes. So, for example, today the journalists, the information is without any kind of control. You are free to express your opinion to convince the public, to inform public opinion about cases of corruption and so on. It is a phenomenon that was not seen before, because everybody was afraid to express his own opinion in public.

So there are different forms of the rediscovered human dignity which the people of Ukraine are manifesting in today's circumstances.

Apologists for Russia sometimes boast that Russia is saving herself from the liberalizing trends that the West seems to be embracing. It is, they say, a true Christian nation serving as a bulwark against decadence, filth, immorality, and the like. Ukraine, on the other hand, embraces Western liberalism and wants to be part of the European Union. This is what led to the Revolution of Dignity, after all. Are there pressures for Ukraine to allow things such as gay marriage, physician-assisted suicide, gender ideology, and the like?

I would not believe that in today's circumstances, a state, by its paternalistic protection of the Church, is able to foster Christian values. The reality is that very often the state will instrumentalize religion and the Christian Church for its own political or geopolitical proposals. And that is exactly what is happening in Russia.

If you compare the dimension of abortion in Russia with abortion in Holland or Belgium, the most liberal countries of western Europe, you will see that Russia has many times exceeded the number of abortions than those liberal countries. If you count how many people on Easter Sunday go to church in Russia and compare the number of people going to church in France, you will see that Russia is an even more liberal country, more affected by Western immorality than some ancient Western democracies.

Of course, Ukraine as a new democracy is exposed to the different viruses coming from around the world. Especially today, Ukraine looks like an open wound, and in the open wound many kinds of flies will come to sit and try to lay their eggs.

But it is our duty, as Christians in Ukraine, to witness Christian values. I believe that there is no Europe without Christian values and there is no European perspective without Christian roots. And the most important European values — such as the dignity of the human person, the common good, solidarity, subsidiarity, and private initiatives — are the cornerstone of the social doctrine of the Church. And I think that Ukraine has a special mission, not only to foster that social doctrine and to build on those cornerstones in our society, but also to help Western Europe, toward which we are oriented right now, to rediscover its own Christian roots. I think that collusion between Church and state will damage the Church, but strong witness of Christian values inside a democratic, open society will give the Church authenticity.

It is why I am Christian, I'm Catholic, fostering the European culture in Ukraine today.

In 2019, we commemorated the thirtieth anniversary of the fall of the Berlin Wall. In those years when the Soviet Empire was crumbling, we thought that atheistic communism was defeated. But today, we are experiencing the loss of the sense of the transcendent, especially in Western societies. It's almost as if communism has won that battle. We have seen an increasing number of Nones, people who affiliate with no religion. What are some of our challenges as a Church to respond to, and what do we have to offer?

I think we are witnessing the emergence of a new global culture, which according to the expression of Archbishop Salvatore Fisichella,[4] it looks like a fog, which you can see but cannot touch, and that fog is an obstacle to see the perspective. That is the phenomenon of a new globalized culture. But that fog will not exist forever; it will condense. And that globalization is a challenge for a new evangelization, because we have to refill with the word of the Gospel each human situation in which we live.

---

4. President of the Pontifical Council for Promoting the New Evangelization.

For example, each day I have to renew my faith, my Christian commitment, my contact with God. If I move to another city, I have to find in that new place a space for prayer, for communion and for my relationship with God. So I have to reevangelize my own personal situation each day and in each place.

The same is happening worldwide, with the creation of a new global culture. And that globalization in itself is neutral, a new possibility, a new challenge for the mission of the Church. But in this new emerging global culture, we as Christians are supposed to be present, to bring to that culture the word of God. If the Church is the continuation of the Incarnation of Christ in today's human history, our task is to incarnate the divine word into that culture.

Second, a human being is always a religious being. Maybe the way to express one's religiosity can change. A way to even understand that we do have religious dimensions will come. I remember that in the Synod on Youth, it was clearly underlined that young people are very religious today. But maybe the way to express and to live their religiosity is drastically different from the way their grandparents or parents did. But their demand and expectation for transcendence is increasing. And we can hear the words of Saint Paul in the new circumstances: "But who will believe if nobody preaches? Who will become Christian if nobody preaches our Lord Jesus Christ dead and risen?" (see Rom 10:14).

So there is not a new circumstance by itself atheistic. No, it depends on which kind of meaning, which kind of religious life will fill the new circumstances. Maybe we find ourselves in the same circumstances as in the marriage in Cana: People would come to Christ saying, "There is no more wine. The jars are empty" (see Jn 2:3). What are you supposed to do? Well, according to the words of Mary, we have to obey the words of Jesus Christ. We have to refill them with water, the material that we do have, and trust that he will do his part. He will change that water into the outstanding wine that will be given at the very last moment.

This is my absolute conviction and belief, because I remember the circumstances of the Soviet Union. I can compare today's new secularist situation on the global level when I hear those complaints about the irrelevance of religion for today's man. I feel like I'm living some sort of déjà vu.

It already happened.

But you will see that one day, that identity of human beings as a religious being will suddenly erupt, as it did at the end of the Soviet Union. The flourishing of religious life in Ukraine right now is some sort of compensation, a reaction to the oppressive policy of the Soviet state, oppression of that human religious reality. That oppression passed, and that need for a big compensation suddenly erupted.

So human beings are always the same: yesterday, today, and tomorrow. And Saint Paul says that Jesus Christ is always the same: yesterday, today, and forever. But we as Christians should not be afraid to witness to our Faith, because the world needs the hope that only we can bring to humanity. Hope comes not from welfare, not from a secure international policy, not from the culture of success, but from faith in the living Christ. He is the source of hope for every human being in this world.

12

At the Foot of the Cross

Sviatoslav Shevchuk never imagined that he would lead his Church during wartime, as Metropolitan Andrei Sheptytsky did during the first and second world wars. But on February 24, 2022, he was thrust into such a position.

The Russian invasion of Ukraine fell — according to the calendar of the Eastern Catholic and Eastern Orthodox Churches — a week and a half before the beginning of Lent. The Great Fast — Byzantine Christians' term for the long period of preparation for Easter — began on Monday, March 7.

"For our people, in Ukraine and abroad, it would seem that the Cross of Our Lord was abruptly thrust upon our shoulders from the very beginning of Great Lent, and we have already been carrying it not for a day or two, a week or two, but continuously, day and night," the head and father of the Ukrainian Greek Catholic Church wrote in his Easter pastoral letter for 2022. "For us, Holy Friday has become our daily bread, our everyday reality, and we do not know when the glorious day of victory over evil, hate, and violence will come. However, precisely today Our Lord calls on us to have no doubt in the victory of light over darkness, life over death, truth over falsehood, and He assures us of His love and grace."

Ukrainian Catholics and Orthodox would still greet one another on Pascha, or Easter, with the traditional greeting, "Christ is risen! Indeed He is risen." But for how long the "long Lent" of war would last in Ukraine was anyone's guess. Months of threats and massive Russian military buildup along Ukraine's borders — as well as veiled nuclear threats from Russian President Vladimir Putin, seemingly designed to keep the West from sending their own troops in — led many observers to predict that Putin's forces would oust Ukraine's central government within days. But the determination of Ukrainians to preserve their freedom — helped along by weapons supplied by the US and other western nations — turned the Russians back from the capital and its environs.

Nevertheless, in the first hours and days of the invasion, Kyivans fled to basements, bomb shelters, and metro stations. The subway system was constructed largely during the Cold War, when Ukraine was part of the Soviet Union, and some stations were meant to double as bomb shelters in case of attack from the United States. Now they protected Ukrainians from the heir of their old rulers.

His Beatitude Sviatoslav opened the Cathedral of the Resurrection of Christ, on the east side of Kyiv, to hundreds of people seeking shelter. But Sviatoslav himself could not stay long in his own cathedral. He was one of many political, civic, and religious leaders who would be targeted for elimination if the Kremlin was successful with plans of regime change. Those on "Putin's hit list" were people who would lead a strong resistance to any takeover of the country. Days before the invasion, the United States informed the United Nations that it had credible information showing that Moscow was compiling lists of Ukrainians "to be killed or sent to camps following a military occupation," *The Washington Post* reported.[1] Even before February 24, there were Russian agents in Kyiv ready to carry out orders. Sviatoslav told me in June 2022 that some of them had already joined the cathedral youth group and choir. In the

---

1. John Hudson and Missy Ryan, "U.S. Claims Russia Has List of Ukrainians 'To Be Killed or Sent to Camps' Following a Military Occupation," *The Washington Post*, February 21, 2022, https://www.washingtonpost.com /national-security/2022/02/20/ukraine-russia-human-rights/.

interview, below, conducted four months into the war, he explained how the threat was neutralized.

And so, for a time, he stayed in an undisclosed location in Kyiv. It was here that he began a daily practice of issuing video messages to let the world know that he was still alive and to lead the Church in prayer. The daily videos also gave Sviatoslav a chance to offer lessons on the Faith — teachings, he said, that would help people endure the hardships of war with Christian dignity. He began with an overview of the Beatitudes. Later, he reviewed Church teachings about sin and repentance and, around the time of Pentecost, reflected on the gifts of the Holy Spirit.

The daily catechetical sessions gave His Beatitude the chance to demonstrate how relevant Christian doctrine still is in today's world. Against a backdrop where an aggressive, better-armed Russia invaded its neighbor without provocation, and where outrageous war crimes were being carried out, Sviatoslav commented that in a modern, "post-truth" culture, good and evil have become confused. People do not see the difference between what gives life and what kills, and sometimes those in power lay false claim to the truth, while those who stand for the truth pay for it with their lives.

"The Ukrainian struggle, the war in Ukraine, poses deep moral questions to the world, which show that one can never call evil good, and good evil," Sviatoslav said.[2]

Months later, he found that he was still working to clarify issues amid the fog of war. "Ukraine holds firm. Ukraine is fighting. Ukraine is fighting for its freedom," he said as Kyiv struggled to fend off a complete Russian takeover of Ukraine's eastern Donbas region.

> But what is freedom? In fact, what is the meaning of our fight? We think of this question from the point of view of the invisible battle, this spiritual struggle that every Christian wages against evil, against the devil, the enemy of the human race. And we know that when we talk about freedom, we are talking about man's ability to

2. The UGCC Department of Information, "Head of the UGCC: The War in Ukraine Shows the World That One Can Never Call Evil Good, and Good Evil," Information Resource of Ukrainian Greek-Catholic Church, March 26, 2022, archived at the Internet Archive, https://web.archive.org/web/20220326134057/http://news.ugcc.ua/en/news/the_war_in_ukraine_shows_the_world_that_one_can_never_call_evil_good_and_good_evil__the_head_of_the_ugcc_96245.html/.

do good. It is not the ability to choose between good and evil, but the ability to multiply the good that the Lord God places in the hands of man. And this is the essence, the content of the Christian ascetic life, it is the struggle against bad thoughts, against passions, it is this work on oneself in order to acquire virtues, certain capacities, those of a person to skillfully do good.[3]

As the Fathers of the Church taught, to be free from sin it is necessary to be aware of one's sinful state, then to oppose this state, and to not follow one's bad inclinations. "It would seem that so often today we might consider that true freedom is inherent to our passions and lusts," His Beatitude said. "And the worst thing you can say to a person who has fallen into the bondage of sin is, 'Well, that's the way you are, the way you were born.'"

"Today, some say that there seems to be a certain right to be a sinner, to do evil, a right to live according to one's wishes," he continued. "We see how this type of artificial rights, this type of indulgence in sinful desires, leads to death. Because they tolerate the killer so he can kill more."[4]

***

Sviatoslav's time was not simply taken up in preaching. As Ukraine's President Volodymyr Zelenskyy rallied his troops to fight and his foreign affairs people to secure more Western support, Sviatoslav kept in touch with the priests and bishops around the country, particularly those on the front lines. Most were staying with their people, he reported.

From its headquarters in Kyiv, the Church coordinated the flow of humanitarian aid to hotspots and tried to help those fleeing war to reach relatively safe Western Ukraine and countries in Eastern Europe. With the death toll mounting and with a third of the country's population displaced, either internally or as refugees in foreign countries, there was

---

3. Video Message of His Beatitude Sviatoslav, July 6, 2022. Transcript available at "Video-Message of His Beatitude Sviatoslav: July 6, 133th [*sic*] Day of the War," Information Resource of Ukrainian Greek-Catholic Church, July 6, 2022, http://news.ugcc.ua/en/articles/videomessage_of_his_beatitude_sviatoslav_june_6_133_th_day_of_the_war_97355.html.

4. "Video Message of His Beatitude."

much work to be done.

After Russian troops withdrew from the center of the country, His Beatitude began visiting places that they had occupied, such as Bucha, Kharkiv, and Poltava. There, he said, "I saw victims of Russian torture and bombing."

The Major Archbishop of Kyiv-Halych also paid visits to military chaplains and hospitals.

In a March 29 meeting, he reported to Kyiv mayor and former heavyweight boxing champion Vitaliy Klitschko that all the Catholic parishes in the city were functioning. Each of them had become a bomb shelter or a center of social service, where priests and faithful were taking care of the elderly and those in need of special care or assistance.

***

Sviatoslav also stayed in close contact with Pope Francis, who called him on the third day of the invasion (just after the pope made an impromptu visit to the Russian Embassy in Rome in a desperate appeal for peace).

On March 25, the day Pope Francis consecrated Ukraine and Russia to the Immaculate Heart of Mary from the Vatican, His Beatitude and the Synod of Bishops of the Ukrainian Greek Catholic Church gathered in the Catholic Marian shrine of Zarvanytsia in Western Ukraine to pray in union with the Holy Father. In comments afterwards, the Major Archbishop told the faithful that the war is a spiritual struggle between good and evil and that the consecration would be the moment when — the faithful believe — good would triumph through the prayers of the Mother of God.

Sviatoslav drove to Lviv in Western Ukraine on March 8 to welcome the papal almoner, Cardinal Konrad Krajewski. As one of two cardinals the pope sent to Ukraine, Cardinal Krajewski wanted to report back to Francis on the humanitarian situation.

In May, His Beatitude received Archbishop Paul Gallagher, the Vatican's Secretary for Relations with States, at the cathedral in Kyiv.

But the Ukrainian spiritual leader did not hesitate to express his disappointment about certain attitudes taken by the Church in the West toward the struggle between Ukraine and Russia. When it became known, for example, that the annual Good Friday Way of the Cross held in Rome's Colosseum would include a prayer co-written by a Ukrainian woman and a Russian woman, who would share the action of carrying the cross, Sviatoslav called the decision "untimely." Apparently, Vatican planners meant it as a gesture of hope for reconciliation, a prayer for peace between the two warring nations. But Ukrainians saw it as insensitive, to say the least.

"When we saw [the text of the Good Friday meditation written by the Ukrainian and Russian women] in the context of that intense phase of the war, after all the horrific acts of genocide against our people, after I visited our towns and villages that were under short-lived but deadly occupation, I realized that something was wrong," he told the Ukrainian online news outlet *NV.* "And we communicated that idea very intensively, to change something. Some things were changed, others were not."[5]

In the end, the women would still share the carrying of the cross, but their prayer would not be read aloud during the ceremony.

If it were meant to serve as a gesture of reconciliation, His Beatitude wanted the Vatican to understand that reconciliation between two peoples at war "is a long-term process of healing." Before that process could even begin, certain conditions would have to be met.

"The first condition would be: you must stop killing us," he said in the *NV* interview. "We can't speak of healing wounds while the enemy is still constantly wounding you. In order to reconcile, you have to be alive. That's why I called this idea 'untimely,' not bad or erroneous, but untimely. In order to achieve reconciliation in the future, we all need to work very hard. And until this is done, it is not yet the time to discuss verbal or dramatized acts of reconciliation, particularly between the Ukrainian and Russian people."

"A second factor, without which there can be no beginning of reconciliation, is condemning criminal acts, in order to achieve justice for the victim," he continued, explaining that reconciliation between Poles and

---

5. Transcript of the interview is available at "We Christians Have a Special Mission — to Transform a Natural Feeling of Anger — to Courage — His Beatitude Sviatoslav in an Interview with NV," Information Resource of Ukrainian Greek-Catholic Church, April 27, 2022, http://news.ugcc.ua/en/articles /we_christians_have_a_special_mission__to_transform_a_natural_feeling_of_anger__to_courage__his_beatitude _sviatoslav_in_an_interview_with_nv_96634.html.

Germans would not have been possible if the Nuremberg Trials had not been conducted in the wake of the Second World War, "and if Nazism as an ideology had not been condemned."

"In our situation, any dialogue on reconciliation between Ukrainians and Russians can only take place when the Nuremberg Trials are conducted over the present murderous ideology."

***

The ideology to which he referred is that of the Russian World (*Russkiy Mir*), which served as a philosophical underpinning of Russia's invasion of its neighbor. In the wake of the February 24, 2022, military action, the Orthodox Christian Studies Center at Fordham University issued "A Declaration on the 'Russian World' (*Russkiy Mir*) Teaching," in which it defined the ideology succinctly:

> The teaching states that there is a transnational Russian sphere or civilization, called Holy Russia or Holy Rus', which includes Russia, Ukraine and Belarus (and sometimes Moldova and Kazakhstan), as well as ethnic Russians and Russian-speaking people throughout the world. It holds that this "Russian world" has a common political centre (Moscow), a common spiritual centre (Kyiv as the "mother of all Rus"), a common language (Russian), a common Church (the Russian Orthodox Church, Moscow Patriarchate), and a common patriarch (the Patriarch of Moscow), who works in "symphony" with a common president/national leader (Putin) to govern this Russian world, as well as upholding a common distinctive spirituality, morality, and culture.[6]

A central figure in the promotion of the Russian World ideology is Patriarch Kirill of Moscow, the head of the Russian Orthodox Church. Kirill was widely criticized for not speaking out against the invasion — and, in fact, seeming to give it his blessing. Pope Francis, in a video conference

---

6. "A Declaration on the 'Russian World' (*Russkii Mir*) Teaching," *Public Orthodoxy*, March 14, 2022, https://publicorthodoxy.org/2022/03/13/a-declaration-on-the-russian-world-russkii-mir-teaching/.

with the Patriarch, warned him not to become "Putin's altar boy."

His Grace Metropolitan Borys Gudziak, archeparch of Philadelphia, said in an interview with Aid to the Church in Need: "Patriarch Kirill has developed this ideological construct called the 'Russian world,' which basically says, wherever we had our empire, that's our canonical territory, and we are the predominant Church that is supposed to guide society and have its footprint there. This phrase, 'Russian World,' was then taken from the Church by Putin and is now being used by him."[7]

For his part, Sviatoslav lambasted comments the Moscow Patriarch made at the Thirtieth International Educational Readings held in the Kremlin in May. Sviatoslav considered it "outrageous" that Kirill "called on teachers of the basics of Orthodox culture to educate children by using the examples of so-called heroes who are fighting in Ukraine today and allegedly defending Russia with weapons in their hands."[8]

Catholics and members of the autocephalous Orthodox Church of Ukraine were not the only ones condemning Kirill for publicly siding with the Kremlin during the "special military operation," as Putin called the invasion. Even parishes of the Ukrainian Orthodox Church that were still under the Moscow Patriarchate began to distance themselves from the Russian Orthodox Church. Indeed, the stance of the Patriarch of Moscow threatened serious implications for Orthodox relations and for ecumenical relations between the Orthodox and Catholic Churches.

Speaking through Zoom to a May 23 conference, "Ukraine: Tasks for Peace-Building," organized by the Ambrosianeum Foundation in cooperation with the Catholic University and Archdiocese of Milan, Italy, His Beatitude Sviatoslav appealed to the academic community to "investigate and condemn the ideology of the 'Russian World,' which aims to resolve the Ukrainian question in the same way that the Nazis wanted a solution

---

7. "Russia Has Ukrainian Greek Catholic Church in the Crosshairs," Aid to the Church in Need, March 14, 2022, https://www.churchinneed.org/russia-has-ukrainian-greek-catholic-church-in-the-crosshairs/.

8. The UGCC Department of Information, "From the Head of the UGCC on Day 90: God Save and Protect Us from Such an Orthodox Culture as Russia's," Information Resource of Ukrainian Greek-Catholic Church, May 25, 2022, http://news.ugcc.ua/en/news/from_the_head_of_the_ugcc_on_the_90th_day_of_the_war_god_save_and_protect_all_people_from_such_an_orthodox_culture_as_russia_96939.html.

to the Jewish question."[9]

As evidence, he pointed to a manifesto published on the website of RIA Novosti, a Russian state-owned news agency, where "the first paragraph declares that Ukrainian as a nationality does not exist; that Ukrainians are Russians who have come to believe that they are Ukrainian. There is no Ukrainian history, language, or culture."

"As a people, we were condemned to annihilation," he summed up.

The Major Archbishop compared the Russian World ideology to the doctrine of the Islamic State, the jihadist group that had taken over parts of Iraq and Syria almost a decade earlier. "The same arguments are used, but cloaked in Christian robes," he said. The ideology supports a "metaphysical war against universal globalism" and considers the Ukrainian people to be "under the influence of the morally degenerate West, presented as the Antichrist. And so, Ukrainians are the ones who carry the seeds of the Antichrist, and must therefore be killed."

Charging that rape is used as a weapon in the war against Ukraine, Sviatoslav said that sexual crimes are mostly committed in public — in order to humiliate the victim. That, he said, is the "true face" of *Russkiy Mir*.

"We are talking about religious fundamentalism of a totalitarian nature, of which we are victims," he said.

✳✳✳

After Russian troops withdrew from Kyiv and its surrounding towns, apparently to pursue a better strategy in concentrating their forces in Donbas, Ukrainians began discovering mass graves and evidence of Russian war crimes. Civilians, particularly those who were helping the Ukrainian Army to defend their own country, and those who were likely to be leaders in a resistance, seemed to be targeted. Sviatoslav paid visits to Bucha, where he prayed over a mass grave in the yard of an Orthodox church, and the other towns near Kyiv that had been briefly

---

9. See The Secretariat of the Head of the UGCC in Rome, "Russia's War Crimes Are Ukraine's Genocide, Says UGCC Head at Milan Conference," Information Resource of Ukrainian Greek-Catholic Church, May 26, 2022, http://news.ugcc.ua/en/news/the_crimes_of_the_russian_army_in_ukraine_are_the_genocide_of_our _people__head_of_the_ugcc_at_the_conference_in_milan_96946.html.

but violently occupied: Irpin and Hostomel.

His Beatitude also joined his voice to the worldwide condemnation of other atrocities carried out by the Russian military: aerial bombing of civilian sites such as the maternity hospital and drama theater in the long-besieged city of Mariupol; missile strikes on crowded train stations, open air markets, and shopping malls — not to speak of the hundreds of apartment buildings that have been hit. Indeed, the Church's own humanitarian aid agency Caritas came under fire in Mariupol, with the loss of seven lives, including two staff workers. Sviatoslav appealed for humanitarian corridors into and out of Mariupol, where some people resorted to drinking water out of radiators because the infrastructure had been destroyed. He asked Ukrainian Catholic priests and bishops worldwide to conduct memorial services for those buried in mass graves without Christian prayer and burial.

On another occasion, he voiced concern about a Kremlin plan to depopulate Ukraine, apparently as part of a Russification of the land.

"They are trying to do everything possible to get as many Ukrainians as possible to leave their land," the Major Archbishop said in late May. "The occupiers are evicting Ukrainians from their homes or destroying the houses that their weapons can reach. They have already deported more than a million from the occupied territories."[10]

Indeed, in July, the *New York Times* reported on the existence of so-called "filtration camps" set up by the Putin regime, where Ukrainians with ties to the military and other civilians deemed a threat to Russian rule would be taken, interrogated, tortured, and sent to remote places in Russia, as far as Siberia.[11]

***

By the time this manuscript was completed, the future looked challeng-

---

10. Transcript available at The UGCC Department for Information, "From the Head of the UGCC on the 91st Day of the War: A Blatant Crime Is Happening in Ukraine — the Russian Occupiers Are Pursuing a Policy of Depopulating Ukraine," Information Resource of Ukrainian Greek-Catholic Church, May 27, 2022, 2022, http://news.ugcc.ua/en/news/from_the_head_of_the_ugcc_on_the_91st_day_of_the_war_a_blatant_crime_is _happening_in_ukraine__the_russian_occupiers_are_pursuing_a_policy_of_depopulating_ukraine_96963.html.

11. "The U.S. Identified 18 Russian 'Filtration Camps' for Ukrainians, a Diplomat Says," *New York Times*, July 11, 2022.

ing, if not bleak. As Ukraine faces an uncertain future, the question of the Church's survival under a possible Russian occupation is one to consider. Recent history does not allow for optimism. As some media have reported, the eight-year-long war in Donbas prior to 2022, as well as the Russian occupation of Crimea, already presented challenges for the Catholic Churches — both Byzantine and Latin. Some priests were forced to leave their parishes, even before the major invasion of 2022.

In 2014, the human rights organization Forum 18 reported that a Polish priest, Fr. Piotr Rosochacki, who had worked in Crimea for five years, was forced to leave the peninsula. He had served as senior priest of Assumption of the Blessed Virgin Mary parish in Simferopol. This was the first of several "casualties" for the Catholic Church, as well as for other religions, due to Russia's Federal Migration Service's refusal to renew residence permits for foreign citizens who were working for local religious communities in Crimea. Yana Smolova of Russia's Federal Migration Service in Crimea told Forum 18 News Service that only registered religious communities can invite foreign citizens.[12]

Greek Catholic priests serving Crimean parishes were told they could remain for only three months at a time, before having to leave for three months.

In Donbas, Auxiliary Bishop Jan Sobilo of the Kharkiv-Zaporizhia Latin Catholic diocese, said in 2022: "There hasn't been a Holy Mass in Luhansk for two years, because Roman Catholic priests are not allowed there. I wanted to go there by myself, but my request was refused."[13]

As the six-month anniversary of the invasion approached in August 2022, the autocephalous Orthodox Church of Ukraine reported that dozens of its priests had been kidnapped or killed, the *Wall Street Journal* said.[14]

All of this seems consistent with the ideology of *Russkiy Mir*, where the spiritual care of a greater Russia would be served primarily by the Russian Orthodox Church.

---

12. Felix Corley, "CRIMEA: 'All Our Priests and Nuns Will Have to Leave by the 2014 Year End,'" Forum 18, November 3, 2014, https://www.forum18.org/archive.php?article_id=2012.

13. Anatolii Babynskyi, "'We Are with Our People' — Pastoral Ministry in Ukraine's War Zones," *The Pillar*, May 14, 2022, https://www.pillarcatholic.com/we-are-with-our-people-pastoral-ministry/.

14. Ian Lovett, "Ukrainian Clergy Say Russian Occupiers Target Them with Threats, Violence," *Wall Street Journal*, August 13, 2022, https://www.wsj.com/articles/ukrainian-clergy-say-russian-occupiers-target-them-with-threats-violence-11660377935?page=1.

The Russian occupation "would obliterate Ukraine's religious freedom, by design," religious freedom expert John Smith told the Religious Freedom Institute in June 2022. "We already know that because of vivid proof from the territory Russia has controlled since its 2014 invasion of Crimea and Donbas: religious organizations have been destroyed or driven out, clergy murdered or imprisoned, and religious buildings desecrated or damaged. Since February's invasion, abundant evidence has emerged that Russian forces are repeating this devastation on a larger scale in the new territory it occupies."[15]

If Orthodox Russia cannot tolerate other Orthodox — because they belong to the Orthodox Church of Ukraine, a Church that is not affiliated with the Moscow Patriarchate — what hope can there be for the Ukrainian Greek Catholic Church? His Beatitude Sviatoslav did not seem to wish to make any predictions when I spoke with him in June 2022. "We will see," he said. But he knows that the Church has been on the cross before — and yet experienced resurrection. He himself lived through it. Those who suffered for the Faith during Soviet times were his teachers, and so many Ukrainians — Catholic and Orthodox alike — had also learned vital lessons at the foot of the cross.

Perhaps no words from the Gospel, then, meant more to Ukrainian Christians in 2022 — and now — than those of Jesus, who said, "Whoever wishes to come after me must deny himself, take up his cross, and follow me" (Mt 16:24).

Here then is our last conversation:

John Burger: Your Beatitude, would you give us an overview of your experience since the war started on February 24? How has the war changed your daily life and routine?

His Beatitude Sviatoslav: First of all, I have to say that the war in Ukraine started eight years ago, but it was mostly in the Eastern part of Ukraine. On the twenty-fourth of February, the war hit us directly here in the capital of Ukraine, because Kyiv was the main direction, the main goal of the

---

15. John Smith, "Why Ukraine Is So Resilient, and Why It Must Win — The Religious Freedom Factor," Religious Freedom Institute, May 18, 2022, https://religiousfreedominstitute.org/why-ukraine-is-so-resilient-and-why-it-must-win-the-religious-freedom-factor/.

Russian troops. They moved down from Russia, from Belarus, through the Chernobyl zone and entered into the neighborhoods of Kyiv very quickly. So in five or six hours, the tanks were twenty kilometers from our cathedral. So basically, Kyiv was almost encircled by the Russian troops.

They were also trying to land big aircraft with paratroopers, and they were trying to conquer two places around Kyiv: Hostomel and Vasylkiv, just to trap us in a circle. The left side of the Dnipro River, where the cathedral is located, was almost entrapped, because they were moving on land from the site of the city of Brovary; that is, they were stopped almost twenty kilometers from the cathedral to the east of Kyiv. But they were also trying to enter the city from the north with specially trained troops to overtake the capital and destroy the central government. In such a way, they were planning to dominate Ukraine when the capital fell, so everything else would be under Russian control.

But thanks be to God, they were stopped. All that time I was here; I was in Kyiv. The first reaction was a big shock, because you can never imagine how dramatically such a beautiful and large city can change. All bridges were closed, and there was almost zero possibility to move through the city. There were some days when it was absolutely forbidden to go out of your house. Immediately, grocery stores, pharmacies were closed, and for many of the people it was almost impossible to find food — in such a big city as Kyiv.

But the biggest danger was from the sky, because Kyiv was bombed by aircraft, with missiles, with artillery. And people were supposed to be down in the air raid shelters. Our cathedral was immediately converted into such a shelter. Each day we protected almost five hundred people in the crypt. We stayed together. We were aware that we are responsible for those people, for their lives. We started to organize special logistics to provide food, to provide medicine, to provide everything the people needed in order to stay there, because it was February, and it was cold. It was not easy to keep so many people warm.

We learned a lot. First, we learned how to discern various kinds of military sounds. Is it the sound of an airplane or a helicopter? Is it the noise of cannon, missile, or artillery? Are they shelling us, or is the Ukrainian Army shelling them?

So it was a very tough moment. But thanks be to God, we survived.

Was there any point at which you thought you might die?

It was clear from the very beginning, because Russians were present in Kyiv far ahead of the 24th of February. They infiltrated even the youth groups of the parish community at the cathedral. Even the choir. They had very precise orders with a list of people to eliminate, with their addresses. And those assault groups were moving around the city very quickly. And I was told by foreign ambassadors that I was on the list.

Why would you be on that list?

Well, I don't know, but afterwards, when the Russians were expelled from the environs of Kyiv, and we started to rediscover the mass graves and we listened to the witnesses of these atrocities, it was the same question: "Why? Why would Russians kill civilians?" We were told that they were asking, "What kind of profession are you in?" If you were a schoolteacher, you would be executed. If you are a sportsman or an artist — painting icons, perhaps — you would be executed. So any kind of expression of national culture, the life of the Ukrainian people, anything that was an expression that Ukrainians are a different nation, [was] supposed to be annihilated. They declared that they had two goals to pursue in Ukraine: to denazify and to demilitarize Ukraine. To *denazify* Ukraine means to kill anything that reminds you of the Ukrainian nation or Ukrainian ethnicity as such. And of course, the Ukrainian Greek Catholic Church is not only a symbol of the Ukrainian nation, but the Church for centuries was almost the only expression of the social life of the Ukrainian people, even if we were living in foreign countries, such as Russia, Poland, the Austro-Hungarian Empire, and so on. And Russians knew very well that the Ukrainian Greek Catholic Church specifically was considered as a soul of the Ukrainian nation. That's why we would be among the first to be eliminated.

Would that list include other bishops, civil leaders, people at the university?

Yes. I could not see those lists, but the ambassadors who [had left Ukraine prior to the invasion and] returned to Kyiv after a few months reported to me very diplomatic information. But I know that on this list was included representatives of other Churches and religious organizations, such as Metropolitan Epiphanius, who is the head of the Orthodox Church of Ukraine, and others.

Everyone who would be considered a danger to the so-called Russian World, a danger to the state ideology, which states that the Ukrainian nation does not exist, that Ukrainians are Russians, but a little heretically oriented, everything that contains the name *Ukraine* should be annihilated, and Ukrainians are supposed to be reeducated. That was a whole plan. And Russian troops were just executing the plan, according to the letter.

It was very interesting that in one media source — RIA Novosti — that manifesto of the Russian plan of denazification of Ukraine was published, and Yale historian Timothy Snyder, who for years was studying the Holocaust in post-Soviet territories, immediately identified it as a manifesto of Ukrainian genocide, made by the Russians. So the ideology started to kill, methodically and with great cruelty.

How was that plot that involved infiltrators in the cathedral choir uncovered and neutralized?

In the very beginning, in the first days, our cathedral was attacked by several assault groups. Even people who were orienting the attacks of Russian missiles were arrested in Kyiv. They would mark buildings, especially government buildings, but also churches, to orient the trajectory of Russian rockets. People of our neighborhood immediately organized themselves into a so-called self-defense group. And each day they were arresting people who were trying to mark our cathedral. They also captured those armed groups that were trying to assault our residence and cathedral.

That started very simply. When so many people were gathered in the crypt of our cathedral, I gave advice to the volunteers to not let anyone bring arms into the shelter, because it could simply be dangerous. They started asking everybody who wanted to enter to show their documents and show their bags, to make sure there were no arms or explosives. And immediately we found people who were trying to enter with arms. Some would obey the orders, and some not. Some of them were using arms in order to attack us. So we asked those self-defense groups for help and protection. In such a way we were forced to organize special places to defend the cathedral. There was some shooting around the cathedral because those people with arms would not obey. But thanks be to God, nobody was injured. But each day some assault group was arrested. They would call this process "collecting mushrooms." Each evening the volunteers and defenders were "collecting mushrooms" around the cathedral. They discovered who they were with documents, special maps, with those lists [of] how to move around and [of] specific orders. And even how they obey or disobey the orders was a sign that those people were trained how to behave if they were detained.

So it was very clear who was who. Some of them had very aggressive tattoos on their bodies, saying "Syria," "Libya," all the places where they already had served before.

The volunteers and members of the self-defense groups would take those *mushrooms* to the representative of the Ukrainian Army and special services who were in charge of defending the capital of Ukraine.

How did it make you feel when you discovered you were on this hit list?

Well, in those first days and weeks we did not think about ourselves, because from the very beginning it was clear that you could be killed at any time. But all our attention was given to the people who were in the cathedral, to the people who stayed in their homes without the possibility to get food, with no electricity, no water, no heat. We were trying to help evacuate people from the city of Kyiv. Before the war erupted, the city counted more or less four million people. In those first two weeks, the majority was evacuated. It was less than one million that remained — mostly men who were recruited into the self-defense groups and the military. Our attention, especially in those first two weeks, was directed to this specific mission to save people's lives.

And also I was impressed how the city system was working: rescue groups, firefighters, ambulances, hospitals. Each day, they were repairing the electricity and water supply and each day recovering people from collapsed buildings. That work was really outstanding, and we were trying to help in any way we could to rescue survivors.

It was really horrible to see how Russians were striking hospitals. They were looking for those places where people would mostly be located, detecting those places through geolocation which your cell phone emits, and especially these assault groups and their collaborators were looking in the hospitals, in order to kill those who were there. Those images of such cruelty were something I cannot forget.

You said in one of your daily video messages that on the first Sunday after the invasion began, pastors were going into the metro system and bomb shelters to serve the Divine Liturgy with the people. Can you tell me about any specific example of that and what it was like?

Because so many assault groups and saboteurs were moving through the city, the very first Saturday and Sunday, a curfew was declared. And of course, we were not able to celebrate our offices in the churches. So we tried to go to those places where people were located. When people cannot go to church, the Church should go to the people. And the metro stations and such bomb shelters as we had beneath our cathedral were places where people were located. It was my appeal, especially to the priests in Kyiv, to descend to those places and be with the people and celebrate the Divine Liturgy there, with them and for them. In the beginning it was very challenging because people were not expecting priests to come. And also it was not quite a holy place to put your things and pray solemnly. But people were not only surprised but very pleased with the presence of the priests. And many of them for the first time of their lives approached for confession. They were asking us to stay, not only for an hour but to stay and be with the people, to preach, to confess. So it was a very unique pastoral moment. I spoke to my priests who did that in different locations in Kyiv. All of them were very excited because of that.

I think that we survived in Kyiv as a city, as a community because of common prayer, because of solidarity, so we withstood. In such circumstances, the presence of priests was a moment when fear was taken away. So we stopped fear, and we looked around us with different eyes, and well, we did well. We expelled our enemies, and not only the city of Kyiv survived, but all that region around Kyiv was liberated.

As you've been going through this ordeal, are you thinking at all about when your Church was in the underground, from 1946 to 1989?

Yes, of course. But it especially reminds me of the Maidan, the so-called Revolution of Dignity of 2013 to 2014, because it was also a moment when all the churches, not only our Church, went out to the streets, to the central square of Maidan, and stood with our people. That was a clear gesture, but also the public space where the Church is supposed to be present, to be with our people. And everything we are doing right now, in different parts of Ukraine, according to the situation, we are staying with our people. Our military chaplains are staying with our soldiers on the front lines. Our monks are staying with our people even in the occupied territories — in great danger. We are staying with our people in the cities of Kharkiv, Odesa, and Mykolaiv, and each day they are living the same thing Kyiv went through in the very beginning of the invasion. But they are there. It's the "sacrament of presence," which is most important. Then we can administer our sacraments of the Church.

But also, all humanitarian aid that we are able to distribute goes through the presence of our Church, because our priests, bishops, monks, and nuns remain in their monasteries and parishes, so we were able to organize this network of the movement of humanitarian aid. And it is increasing each day. But also we were able to be flexible, because very often the situation is changing. Perhaps those territories that were occupied are now liberated, and they have different needs than they had just a month before. We're supposed to heal those wounds. Many people are trying to go back home, because they were forced to leave their cities and villages. We are supposed to be with them and help them. It's not easy to go back:

Your house can be filled with explosives. Many people died going back home, opening their houses, even opening their cars, because Russians would leave traps to kill people even after their withdrawal. To console, to heal the wounds, to serve those who are in extreme need is a mission of the Church, to be with her people.

Our government is warning that the upcoming winter could be the most difficult, most challenging winter in the whole history of Ukraine, because Russians are systematically destroying the infrastructures of the big cities, of the food stores, of the heating system. The cost of food is increasing each day, because often it is not easy — sometimes impossible — to find fuel, to find gasoline or diesel. The transportation of humanitarian aid is becoming more and more expensive. It means that in wintertime we'll be freezing and lacking food supplies. Right now, we are making special efforts to be prepared for the wintertime as much as we can.

You mention a network of monasteries and parishes to facilitate the movement of humanitarian aid. Please give me an example of how that works.

Perhaps I will give you an example of the city of Kherson, which even until now is under Russian occupation. Right now it is impossible to bring humanitarian aid to Kherson from the Ukrainian side. Until last week it was possible to send money to that monastery. They had a bank account, which was still working. It's a miracle. We transferred money, and they were able to receive that money and buy groceries from the local farmers, because Russia would confiscate everything without paying. And those farmers would be very pleased to have a network to sell their products and receive money in order to survive. Our Basilian monastery in Kherson became a humanitarian hub. They would receive the money, buy food from the farm, organize each day the kitchen in their monastery, and thousands of people would come and get food.

I don't know how long it will function.

Another example: our cathedral in Kharkiv. Kharkiv is almost at the front line. Our bishop there, Bishop Vasyl [Tuchapets], is staying there without moving. Each day in our cathedral, two thousand people receive food. Kharkiv is like the last point of this network of the logistics of humanitarian aid. Some buses are constantly going there. In the church there is a big storage of all that stuff, and people each day go there asking for food. In the second month in Kharkiv, they started to experience big problems with the water supply, because when the water system was destroyed by bombs and partially restored, the water was not potable. If people got some food product, they would have to cook it, and without water it's impossible. So the situation that was created was that they received things without the possibility to prepare the food. So the bishop asked for the possibility to provide a water filtration system. We made special efforts, and he did find a big system for water filtration. We brought that to Kharkiv, and just next to the cathedral, they found a pipe, and with the special permission of city authorities opened that water supply. Each day, hundreds of thousands of people with bottles make lines in order to get the water.

I visited Kharkiv a few days ago, and I saw this with my eyes. It makes you cry.

You did your own military service in Luhansk, which is now going through a big struggle, as Putin wants to take over the whole of the Donbas. As one who once served in the military there, what is your estimation of the situation and the possible outcome?

I have mixed feelings, because I had an experience of the Soviet mentality of how to treat their own soldiers and how to achieve military goals.

The first problem is that right now Russians are trying to fulfill some political goals through military means. For example, they receive an order to conquer this city by a certain date, because that is Victory Day in Russia, the ninth of May. And nobody would count how many soldiers die, how many tanks are destroyed, what price the military is supposed to pay in order to fulfill those commands. That is, I would say, a bit absurd, to fulfill some political goal with a military means. That is what we have with this whole Russian invasion. They announce some political proposal, and they say, "We will not count our costs." Which means that with some irrational cruelty with their own soldiers, they will try to fulfill such a political order, such a command.

It's a very sad principle. In such a way, the Red Army, the Russian Army, was fighting the Nazis in the Second World War. It was the policy of the famous Marshal [Georgy] Zhukov. He was explicitly ordering officers to not be merciful to soldiers, saying, "Women will give birth to more." That is diabolical.

The second is, because very often, we are looking for some diplomatic or political way to stop the war, many diplomats or politicians are trying to talk to Mr. Putin, to make some reasoning in the situation, to prevent further escalation of such a stupid conflict — because I think no one in the world of a sane mind would justify such a war. So they would foster a dialogue.

But from my experience in the Soviet Army, this Asiatic way to treat your enemy is something which regards your opponent as very weak. If he'd be trying to talk to you and have a dialogue in order to prevent the violent physical assault, that was almost a rule in the Soviet Army: If there is a conflict between two soldiers, and one of them is starting to talk to the other in order to prevent the violence, the other would consider him as a weak man, as not worth being his friend, not worth it to be even his interlocutor, not worthy to talk to you. Such a dialogue would be understood as an encouragement for this superman to assault you. In such a situation, what was the policy? Before talking, you had to take a chair and hit your opponent over the head. After such a move, you will be the best friends. He would appreciate you very much. He would treat you as a strong man. He would never use violence to assault you anymore. Even more, he would consider you a friend and someone he could trust in a difficult moment. He's going to be your buddy forever.

So maybe for European culture and the European mind that is something strange. But that was how to deal with conflict among the Soviet soldiers. When I analyze how we're trying to avoid any kind of escalation, how we're trying to resolve existing conflicts, using diplomacy without becoming strong — even military — it was like an encouragement and invitation to our opponent to assault us.

That is sad to say, because that is totally not Christian. We as Christians can never encourage any kind of violence or war. Pope Francis, I would say, very eloquently expressed his condemnation of such a war, saying war is always a loss for humanity. War is sacrilegious, especially the war going on right now in Ukraine. It is the biggest stupidity in modern history, and we have to do everything in order to stop the invader and have peace among nations.

What, in your view, is Putin's ultimate goal? Why is he doing this, and what is his end game?

I think he is trying to solve the inner problems of Russia with an external invasion and aggression. Right now, there is a lot of discussion about the causes of such a war. According to our understanding and direct experience of the situation in Ukraine and Russia, in these post-Soviet countries, each nation has its own spiritual and social sicknesses, illnesses. Ukraine as well. Russia has its own. The history of Russia after the fall of the Soviet Union was the history of a humiliated society. They would feel very often an anger against the whole world that they are not able to be at the same stage of economy as other countries. Such envy started to evolve into a very specific ideology. We generally would call it the ideology of the Russian World. That ideology means the extreme Russian nationalism, nationalism that has some sort of Messianic vocation. It's an ideology to try to "make Russia great again."

How to make Russia great again? Not by developing their own greatness, but to humiliate others, to show that we are already great. But others simply are ignoring us.

The political history of Mr. Putin was always linked with some sort of war. He became known in Russia because of the war in Chechnya [1999–2000]. Everyone united in order to withstand an enemy. He was reelected as president because of the war with Georgia [2008]. And right now, he is reappearing as a new emperor — Peter the Great — in order to collect all the lands of so-called historical Russia. And recently he declared that, in his mind, historical Russia is basically the territory of the Soviet Union. So, in order to be in power, in order to appear a strong superman, a successful leader, he desperately needs to have an external enemy. And right now, the collective West, especially the USA, is an excellent enemy, and he is the one who is saving the pride of his nation standing with this world power, in order to make Russia great again. And that is an internal, I would say, mechanism that is constantly pushing this political system to provoke the world, to create new enemies and fight them in order to solve the inner problems of his country. And right now, Ukraine is the victim of such a vision.

But if Ukraine would be subjugated by Russia, tomorrow he will find another victim to invade. Maybe this example would be very cruel, but the predator who is looking for victims always will blame the victim, and he is himself the victim of very strong internal psychological pressure that is constantly pushing him to kill more and more. And he cannot stop until he is contained.

The war against Ukraine is unprovoked. It's not the fault of NATO or the USA or Ukraine itself. The causes of such aggression are inside the illnesses of a post-Soviet Russian society.

So even if NATO was not expanding, even if it had not promised Ukraine that it could one day be a member, this would still be the situation.

Yes. The smaller countries, such as Ukraine or Croatia or Bosnia-Herzegovina or Georgia, are looking to become members of NATO because we are threatened by Russia. If Russia were not threatening aggression, no one would look for membership in NATO. Until now, Ukraine was a neutral country. We by ourselves decided to give up our nuclear weapons, which Ukraine received as a heritage after the fall of the Soviet Union. Russia, with the USA, assured Ukraine of our integrity, our security. We changed our minds only after the invasion of Russia and the occupation of Donbas and Crimea. What are we supposed to do? We have to look for friends in order to withstand, because compared with Russia we are small and weak.

How long do you think this current situation could go on? How will Ukraine emerge from it?

I don't know, sincerely. I fear that at a certain moment it can become a frozen conflict and in a very short period can be reactivated again. So maybe the ongoing and open military escalation will be at the moment when both sides — Ukrainian and Russian — would be exhausted. Then probably the time of diplomacy will come. But if the conflict itself would be frozen, if Russia would not withdraw its troops and Ukraine would not receive control of the occupied zones, I fear that this conflict will be very quickly reactivated, because Russia will recruit new soldiers, get new resources, and attack us again.

So my prayer is that clear reason one day would provide new perspectives, not an inner instinct of aggression but common good. Well, we are praying for peace, for an end of the war. But peace always has to be connected with truth and justice. An unjust and inauthentic peace would be the imitation of peace. My fear is that the very notion of peace in today's world can change its authentic meaning. Peace doesn't mean the simple absence of war. Peace means harmony, fullness of life. We look for victory over the very cause, which can cause new wars. That's why I think it's our duty to be authentic in our thoughts and to tell the truth, even if that truth can be painful for ourselves. Here in Ukraine, we have to be very aware of what is causing the war and how to heal this open wound.

The Russian website Meduza — which is opposed to the Putin regime — reported in early June that the Kremlin is planning to annex the Donetsk, Luhansk, Kherson, and Zaporizhzhia regions of Ukraine and combine them into a single federal district within Russia. How would this affect the Ukrainian Greek Catholic Church's eparchies and parishes that are there? How would it affect religious freedom?

First of all, we would be very limited in our possibilities to act. That would be the best case. But next could be the elimination of our presence. Because in history, each time Russia conquered territory of Ukraine, our Church was destroyed — not immediately, but in the nearest perspective. Such a possibility or such a scenario is a scenario of the frozen conflict. I think that it would be only an intermediate stage, because they would move forward. And that is very dangerous, because people would continue to suffer — on both sides, occupied and reorganized in some sort of pseudo-statehood construction, and in the territory controlled by the Ukrainian state. It would be only a question of time when the next bite of the territory of Ukraine would be taken.

Are you thinking of any kinds of preparations/contingency plans as a Church, especially in the event of a Russian takeover of Ukraine or part of Ukraine?

Our plan is to stay, to be with our people. And then we will see. Because it was our history — a history of martyrdom and resurrection. And that is maybe our mission and duty.

Would you reflect a little on what efforts Pope Francis has been making regarding the war? How often are you in touch with him? Could you reflect on the exchange of insights: things you have learned from him, perhaps things he has learned from what you have told him?

Yes, we are in touch with him often. On the second day of the war, he called me and promised that he would be doing everything he can in order to stop the war. The Holy Father himself is very empathetic with the suffering of the people of Ukraine. But he is very delicate with his expressions, because he believes that through dialogue it is possible to solve such difficult issues. The Holy See is always the place of meeting and dialogue, not the place of military plans. It is what he himself and his collaborators of the Secretary of State are trying to do.

I have to say that the Holy Father is well-informed about what is going on in Ukraine. And we are working on the possibility for him to visit us in Ukraine. He has expressed his willingness to come and visit us. The Holy Father is very strong in his gestures, and his gesture of visiting Ukraine would be a message itself — a message of support, a message of hope for us.

Of course, maybe Ukrainians would be very pleased if he would make some strong political statement, condemning Mr. Putin, condemning Patriarch Kirill, condemning the ideology of the Russian World. But the policy of the Holy See is not condemning but trying to promote an alternative to the war, which is an alternative of reasoning, dialogue.

He suffers a lot that the efforts he was undertaking until now were not successful. So he tried to contact President Putin. He spoke with Patriarch Kirill in a video conference. But with no success. And the Holy Father is suffering because of that. Maybe he thought that it would be a lot easier to stop the Russian aggression through some sort of mediation. But until now it is quite difficult.

The Holy Father is trying to assist us with any kind of humanitarian help. Caritas Internationalis and many bishops' conferences, especially in Europe but also in the US, are helping us on different levels, visiting us in Ukraine.

Six million refugees have already left Ukraine. Most of them are staying in Europe. European nations are receiving our refugees with an open heart, and the Holy Father is encouraging them and thanking them for that. Some refugees are going to the USA and Canada. Such a sensitivity of the Holy Father for refugees: For decades, he has been trying to educate the nations to be friendly and open to them. Right now, it's vital for our people.

What did you think about the pope's decision to consecrate Ukraine and Russia to the Immaculate Heart of Mary? How did this gesture resonate with Ukrainians?

I have to say that politically it was a big question, because any time Ukraine and Russia are brought together it creates some strong reaction, especially among those who don't go to church. But among Catholics, among believers, especially among those who have a special, even mystical perception of the apparition of Fatima, that act of consecration was really profoundly lived and very well-received. Right now, for already three months we have a pilgrimage statue from Fatima, and this statue is going from parish to parish. Thousands of people, day and night, are praying. So it's a big spiritual movement that started with that moment.

Many people are really grateful to the Holy Father for this act [of consecration]. And people really believe that we as Ukraine, as a nation, are in a special divine plan. There is some divine plan for Russia, but also for Ukraine. In those apparitions at Fatima, the word *Ukraine* was not pronounced — maybe because at that time the majority of the territory of Ukraine was included in the Russian state. But when the Holy Father mentioned Ukraine as well as a subject of this divine providence, for people of Ukraine who really believe in God, who really are inside this mystical sensitivity, it was something very strong. They received a very big consolation and hope.

What do you say to those, such as former US Secretary of State Henry Kissinger, who say that Ukraine should be willing to concede some territory in order to facilitate a peace deal?

We consider Ukraine, Ukrainian territory, as an integral part of the body of the Ukrainian nation. You cannot negotiate your hands or your legs, because it's a part of your person. You cannot say, "In order for the predator to stop, cut off your hand and give it to him. Just a hand, and he will stop!" No, that is naïve, and I would say a very dangerous statement, because at that level we have to follow the principles of international law. And if it's licit, possible, for a big country to invade a small country and to cut off some part of the territory, just because they want it, breaking the law of the international mode of coexistence of the nations, I think that will cause big troubles in the whole world. If we break that fundamental principle of the peaceful coexistence of nations, then you will encourage all kinds of criminals to do the same. So be careful.

Finally, Your Beatitude, what are your thoughts about the European Union's decision to grant candidate status to Ukraine?

It was a historical event, very important for free Ukraine. We were very pleased because of this openness of the European Union, but that is only the beginning. It's not a marriage itself, but only the engagement. I hope we will survive until the marriage — as a state, as a nation. And maybe I would repeat the words of Saint Thomas: I will believe only after I touch.

Very often such a political decision can be initiated but never completed. I hope that one day we will fully join as a member of the European Union because it is a matter of the identity of Europe and security of Ukraine. We need that membership because first of all we are a European nation, and second, right now we are dying for European values, for those values which many countries in the West have already forgotten. Thirdly, Ukraine will reactivate the European Union as such, bring a new vibrancy, will show that the EU is not only about the economy but also about principles. The most important principle is human dignity. That will be a very important contribution of Ukraine for the European Union. My feeling is that right now, for its credibility, the EU as a project of peace-building needs Ukraine more than Ukraine needs the EU. But nevertheless, we see that our future is in that family of the European nations.

Acknowledgments

Many people have been important contributors to the success of this book.

First and foremost, I wish to thank His Beatitude Sviatoslav for his willingness to be interviewed, for his availability, and especially for his kind and Christian hospitality when my wife and I visited him in Kyiv. I also thank his secretary, Fr. Oleh Oleksa, and his household staff for their assistance.

The genesis of this book was an idea pitched to me by Fr. Volodymyr Malchyn, head of the Development and Communications Office, and vice-chancellor of the curia of the Major Archbishop of Kyiv-Halych. He too was helpful to us on our visit to Kyiv and in arranging subsequent interviews.

After our stay in Kyiv, we traveled to Lviv and were in good hands with Fr. Roman Oliynyk, who at that time worked in the Church's Development Office and is now a pastor in the Archeparchy of Philadelphia in the United States. Father Roman's skill at interpreting, his bountiful knowledge of history, and especially his untiring care for us in our daily needs was a great help to me in my on-site research.

Others we met in Ukraine who were very helpful included Metropolitan Volodymyr Viytyshyn of Ivano-Frankivsk; Fr. Bohdan Prach, rector of the Ukrainian Catholic University (UCU); Fr. Ihor Boiko, rector of the Holy Spirit Seminary in Lviv; the seminarians at Holy Spirit Seminary; and Svitlana Hurkina, research fellow at the Institute of Church History at UCU.

Preparing to interview His Beatitude involved much study, speaking with experts, and hearing the perspectives of friends and acquaintances who have experienced Ukraine's recent history and life in the diaspora Church. There are many to thank, including Carl Anderson, supreme knight of the Knights of Columbus; Anatolii Babynskyi, research fellow at UCU's Institute of Church History; author Sue Ellen Browder; Fr. Andriy Chirovsky, founder and first director of the Metropolitan Andrey Sheptytsky Institute of Eastern Christian Studies; Deacon Nicholas Denysenko, professor of theology at Valparaiso University; Adam DeVille, editor of *Logos: A Journal of Eastern Christian Studies*; Fr. John Fields, then-spokesman for the Archeparchy of Philadelphia and now deceased; Jack Figel of the Orientale Lumen Foundation; Fr. Peter Galadza, director emeritus of the Metropolitan Andrey Sheptytsky Institute of Eastern Christian Studies; Archbishop Claudio Gugerotti, then–apostolic nuncio to Ukraine; Fr. Cyril Hovorun, professor of ecclesiology, international relations, and ecumenism at Sankt Ignatios Volkhögskola in Stockholm; Fr. Michael Hutsko, pastor of Saints Peter and Paul Ukrainian Catholic Church in Mount Carmel, Pennsylvania; Fr. Wasyl Kharuk, spiritual director at St. Josaphat Ukrainian Catholic Seminary; Alexander B. Kuzma, chief development officer of the Ukrainian Catholic Educational Foundation; Bishop Basil Losten, bishop emeritus of the Eparchy of Stamford, Connecticut; Fr. Paul Luniw, canon lawyer and pastor in the Eparchy of Stamford; Myroslav Marynovych, vice rector of the Ukrainian Catholic University; Fr. Mark Morozowich, dean of the School of Theology and Religious Studies at The Catholic University of America; Fr. David Nazar, SJ, rector of the Pontifical Oriental Institute in Rome; Fr. Vsevolod Shevchuk, pastor of Holy Ghost Church, Akron, Ohio; Andrew Sorokowski, a longtime researcher and writer on matters pertaining to the

Ukrainian Greek Catholic Church; Tetiana Stawnychy, president of Caritas Ukraine; Msgr. John Terlecky of the Eparchy of Stamford, who also helped me with initial editing; Justin K. H. Tse, then-visiting assistant professor, Asian American Studies Program, Northwestern University; Roman Vaskiv and Oksana Rybak, immigrants from Ukraine living in the U.S.; and Irena Yarosevych, Ukrainian-American journalist.

One of those experts deserves a special word of gratitude for writing the Foreword to this book. Myroslav Marynovich, who served many years in the Soviet gulag in Siberia and is the author of The Universe behind Barbed Wire: Memoirs of a Ukrainian Soviet Dissident, emailed me the text in spite of the loss of power throughout his city of Lviv due to Russian bombing in early October 2022.

In addition, many of my fellow parishioners at St. Michael the Archangel Ukrainian Catholic Church in New Haven, Connecticut, especially Myron Melnyk and Paul Zalonski, offered valuable insights from their experience, as well as support and encouragement.

My colleagues at Aleteia.org, where some of the material in this book first appeared, have also been very supportive. A special note of thanks goes to Fr. Patrick Mary Briscoe, OP, the editor at the time.

My thanks also go to Mary Beth Giltner, senior acquisitions editor at Our Sunday Visitor, and the entire OSV team who worked hard to bring this book to life.

Last but not least, I thank my wife, Mariangeles, who has accompanied me throughout this whole journey — literally and metaphorically. Thank you, dear, for your love and prayers. My family of origin, too, has greatly encouraged me in this project. Finally, this is an appropriate time to remember with great love how my parents, now gone home to God, have been my first teachers, not only in the Faith, but in writing too.

About the Author

John Burger is a veteran Catholic journalist who writes for Aleteia.org. A native of New Rochelle, New York, he earned a bachelor's degree in English from Iona University there and a master of arts from Iowa State University. He and his wife, Mariangeles, live in the United States.